Ge... .ed Wragg

# The English Curriculum in Schools

# THE ENGLISH CURRICULUM IN SCHOOLS

Louise Poulson

CASSELL

**Cassell**

Wellington House
125 Strand
London WC2R 0BB
www.cassell.co.uk

370 Lexington Avenue
New York
NY 10017-6550

**British Library Cataloguing-in-Publication Data**
A catalogue record for this book is available from the British Library.


ISBN 0-304-33783-8 (hardback)
        0-304-33782-X (paperback)

Typeset by BookEns Ltd, Royston, Herts.
Printed and bound in Great Britain by
Biddles Ltd, Guildford and King's Lynn

# Contents

# Acknowledgements

Many colleagues and friends gave support and advice in the writing of this book, and in completing the research on which it is based. I am particularly grateful to Martin Hughes, Liz Wood, Sue Wright and Peter Dougill, who read and commented on drafts of the manuscript. I am also grateful to the staff of the schools in London, Devon and Sheffield who participated in the two projects; and to Hilary Radnor, and Rosie Turner-Bisset with whom I collaborated.

# Foreword

When the *Education Matters* series was first launched in the late 1980s, debate about education was completely dominated by the Education Acts of that decade, particularly the 1988 Education Reform Act, which introduced a statutory National Curriculum containing considerable detail, as well as national tests for pupils aged 7, 11 and 14. Since those years the National Curriculum has been reduced in scope and complexity, but the debate about what should be taught and, indeed, how it should be taught has not diminished.

It has been extraordinarily difficult, not only for parents and lay people, but for professionals working in the field, to keep up-to-date with the ideas and the detail of what is involved in particular types of schooling or subject matter being taught. The *Education Matters* series has tried to address directly some of the major topics, to present the issues and concerns authoritatively, but in clear, jargon-free language. All the books in the series have been of particular interest to a wide range of people, whether they are professionally engaged in education, training to become teachers, or lay people, like parents and governors, who want an overview of the field.

The teaching of English and all that goes with it, such as children learning to read and write and the need for a high standard of competence in communicating with others, has been a central issue throughout this century. English teaching has, from time to time, been politically controversial. There have been attempts to prescribe very closely what should be done in English lessons. Louise Poulson's thorough analysis of English teaching, past, present and future, makes a valuable contribution to the debates.

Professor E. C. Wragg, Exeter University

# Introduction

This book provides an introduction to the place of English in the curriculum of British primary and secondary schools. It examines the recent debates and controversies in English which have centred on the English and Welsh National Curriculum and its assessment, and also considers the reasons underlying the seemingly irreconcilable differences about the subject in the school curriculum. English has come to have a central place in the curriculum of all schools. Not only is it a subject in the curriculum, and an accepted body of knowledge, but it is also the chief means through which pupils are initiated into the requirements and practices of formal literacy. Thus the connection between English as a subject and its role in the development of literacy is of crucial importance.

A further aim of the book is to unravel the complex tangle of arguments about English, and to examine where and how differences originate. Views appear to have become extremely polarized in recent years, something that has been encouraged to a large extent by media representations of the issues. The public have been presented with images of progressive teachers blindly adopting unworkable theories at the expense of children's learning. The media have also presented politicians claiming a victory for common sense and the certainties of tradition. These images have been of concern to teachers, and also to many laypersons such as parents and school governors, in whose interests politicians have claimed to be acting. However, what is really at issue is not so much the validity of one approach to teaching English as opposed to another, but rather the different ways of thinking about the purpose of the subject and its content, and also the ways in which knowledge is structured and transmitted from one generation to another. These differences are underpinned by beliefs and value systems. I argue that the debate about English, or any other part of the school curriculum, will always seem confusing and irresolvable until the underlying value systems and beliefs informing the different perspectives are made explicit.

One of the problems with discussion of the school curriculum, and education in general, is that in recent years a particular system of values and a set of beliefs have been presented as universal common sense. This book examines the various levels at which English can be conceptualized, and it relates these to differences in beliefs and values. A further issue is the attachment to tradition and the traditional. In particular, it examines, and calls into question, the equation between so-called tradition and traditional practices and the raising of standards in education and in literacy.

A number of claims have been made by politicians and other public figures in education about the value of tradition in the teaching of English and other subjects. In general, they suggest that success in education is to be achieved through a return to more traditional practices in schools. These are highly questionable assertions, and they are usually unaccompanied by any clear indication of what exactly constitutes traditional methods and practices, and how they differ from those which are non-traditional. Implicitly, the arguments suggest that traditional practice in English teaching includes a focus on whole-class teaching, the inclusion of Shakespeare and other pre-twentieth-century authors in the curriculum, and a return to a more formal style of examination through tests. In relation to English in primary schools, it usually implies more discrete subject teaching, as opposed to a curriculum that integrates different subjects within a topic or theme; more whole-class teaching; and a greater emphasis on sound–symbol correspondence in the initial teaching of reading. The assumption underlying these claims is that teachers and schools are not doing these things, and if they did so children's education and levels of achievement would improve. Yet as this book and other research shows, most teachers and schools actually do these things, although they may not do them in the ways desired by politicians and their advisers. Most recently, there has been pressure for all primary schools to teach English, or more accurately reading and writing, in a uniform way, by following the same macro-strategy for the literacy hour (which, in fact, is voluntary). If teachers' and schools' freedom of choice is to be justified, then there is an even greater need for them to think carefully about what they do, and make clear to parents and other stakeholders the reasons for their practice and philosophy, and how these relate to children's achievements in literacy and language. Underlying the promotion of tradition is a belief that the past was better than the present, that life was more certain, and that there was clear agreement about issues which are now controversial. This view, although seductive, is mistaken: the past was no more certain than today, and if the uncertainties of the past are examined, they reveal similar preoccupations to those of the present.

The arguments in this book draw substantially on empirical data from two research studies on the teaching and assessment of English in primary and secondary schools. The book also draws on research evidence from other sources, such as that of Webster, *et al.* at Bristol (1996) and that of Bridie Raban and her colleagues at Warwick (Raban *et al.*, 1994) concerning primary and secondary teachers' beliefs, priorities and practices about English and literacy in the late 1990s. The book is in two main parts. The first examines controversies about English teaching and identifies how different perspectives relate to underlying differences in beliefs about the purpose and content of English. In Chapter 1, different ideas of how English should be taught are related to the different value systems and beliefs held about knowledge, and about teaching and learning. In Chapter 2, the current debates about English are compared with ways of thinking about the subject in the past. It is apparent that many of the issues with which we are now concerned were also concerns of the past. One of the most important developments in the past decade has been the statutory National Curriculum and assessment framework. Chapter 3 examines the origin and development of the idea of a core curriculum in English. In particular, the role of the Cox Committee, and its recommendations for English within the National Curriculum, is discussed. It is argued that although the Cox recommendations were acceptable to many teachers, who worked hard to implement the new National Curriculum and to integrate it within their own ways of teaching, they were less acceptable to the government of the time. As outlined in Chapter 4, the political interference in the English curriculum of the early 1990s undid much of the conciliatory work of the Cox Committee, and resulted only in a period of considerable disruption for schools.

The second part of the book, Chapters 5 to 9, is concerned with the practicalities of teaching and assessing English in primary and secondary schools, and also draws on research data. Although there are numerous books that deal with the teaching of English in primary schools or secondary schools, there are few that deal with English in both phases of the school system. Chapter 5 examines the teaching and learning of English language, which has been one of the most controversial aspects of the English curriculum. Chapters 6 and 7 outline how English is taught in primary and secondary schools, and the changes that have occurred in the past twenty years or so. Chapter 8 deals with the assessment of English in both primary and secondary schools, in relation to the National Curriculum and to public examinations such as GCSE. The final chapter outlines some of the key issues in English and in the promotion of literacy for the future. These are related to the changing nature of life in the late twentieth century and also the changing nature of literacy and technology.

# 1
# Controversies in English

English is one of the core subjects in the curriculum of both primary and secondary schools. Although it is considered to be such a central subject in the school curriculum, there has nevertheless been debate and controversy about the primary purpose of English, about the most appropriate content for the subject, and about the methods by which it should be taught. In the past twenty-five years, English and its teaching have been the subject of more official inquiries, reports and general political interest than any other subject on the school curriculum. There have been numerous high-profile media controversies at all levels within the education system, including conflicts about reading standards and the teaching of reading in primary schools; about the teaching of English language, particularly grammar and the role of standard English; about the assessment of English in schools; and about the best ways of training and preparing teachers.

Over a long period, the controversies have continued about the same things – something that often perplexes those who are not involved in English teaching, and even many who are. One reason for the continuation of debates is that the differences in assumptions and values informing different perspectives in English are complex. Furthermore, they are not always related solely to the subject. There are deeper underlying concerns which relate to wider social and political issues. At times of rapid social and economic change, which frequently undermines and challenges old certainties and traditions, language tends to become a particular focus for concern (Crowley, 1989), because it is a key means through which people construct and represent social, cultural, ethnic and national identity. What is deemed more or less important in language and literacy gives an indication of the values and priorities of particular societies and eras. Ideas about the nature of language and literacy reflect ideas about the way in which a society should function best. In the late twentieth century, the questions primarily relate to the ways in which English in the school curriculum can ensure that pupils have competence in the kinds of literacy appropriate to an age of electronic technology, and have access to the networks of communication within a global world economy. They also relate to the role of English language and literature in the construction and maintenance of national and cultural identity. This chapter examines some of the ways in which debates about English have been articulated; these relate to its purpose, its content and the ways in which it should be taught. The chapter also examines how different sets of values and beliefs have informed the arguments in primary and secondary schools.

Controversy over English in the school curriculum has been particularly evident since the 1988 Education Reform Act, and the establishment of a National Curriculum and assessment system in England and Wales. In 1989, the report of the Cox Committee (DES, 1989a) made recommendations on the content and structure of English in the National Curriculum for all pupils aged between 5 and 16. The content of English was represented as four related areas: reading, writing, speaking and listening. These spanned both primary and secondary phases of education. In addition, the committee wisely acknowledged that there were differences of opinion about English, and a variety of practices within the teaching of the subject. In order to offer an inclusive National Curriculum, it attempted to categorize and represent the most influential of these opinions and practices. The committee's final report identified five views of English that could be seen as contributing to good practice in the teaching of the subject. For good reasons, it did not identify the main contradictions and incompatibilities between different views. The five views, which are discussed in detail in Chapter 3, were represented as alternatives, each having equal validity. This was reassuring to many people, but represented a simplification of complex issues. However, it was a potentially dangerous simplification because it did not acknowledge that there were at least three different levels at which differences of opinion could be categorized. These included beliefs about the primary purpose of English, beliefs about its content, and beliefs relating to the nature of knowledge.

Although the Cox Committee recommendations were accepted and supported by most teachers of English, they proved, in the longer term, to be less acceptable to the politicians who had initiated the reform, and also to their successors, who appeared to have an even less inclusive agenda. Between 1990 and 1995 the English curriculum and assessment procedures for primary and secondary schools were the subject of substantial revision and rewriting – a process which led to dispute and open revolt among English teachers and parents against government proposals for assessment, which were considered to be both narrow and dogmatic. The disputes between the Conservative government and teachers, parents, school governors and other interested parties were, on the surface, about English in the National Curriculum and its assessment; however, underlying them were fundamentally different assumptions, values and priorities. The government of the time had undertaken large-scale reform of education, arguing that the reforms were what parents wanted and represented common-sense views of education. However, as the reforms were implemented, it became clear that the aims and values of ministers were increasingly at odds with those of the stakeholders in education and that the ministers concerned were unable to see, or understand, whence those differences originated. This chapter examines some of the important areas of difference in beliefs and values about the purpose of English, about its content and about knowledge and learning.

### The purpose of English

One of the central issues in all the debates about English has been its purpose in schools: in short, what it is for. On the one hand, there are people who believe that its primary purpose is functional: to teach the basic skills of reading and writing, including handwriting, spelling, grammar and punctuation, and to prepare young people for their adult roles as citizens and employees. In contrast, there are others who regard the primary purpose of English in the school curriculum as being the development of pupils' intellectual abilities and their emotional and imaginative expression, as well as the cultivation of moral, cultural and aesthetic values. A more radical view is that it should help pupils to understand the society and culture in which they live, and to be able to identify how they might have a role in shaping and changing it.

The need for clarity about the purpose of English was highlighted in the 1988 report of the Kingman Committee. At the end of this document, there is a 'Note of reservation' from one of the members, Professor Henry Widdowson. He argued that the report had failed to do one very important thing – address the question of why English was on the school curriculum: 'it [the Kingman Report] does not come to grips with the central question of how knowledge about language can be shown to be relevant to the educational aims of English as a school subject' (DES, 1988, p. 77). He further argued that the report did not engage with the issue of how different groups of people had potentially conflicting ideas about its purpose; and that it had, implicitly, highlighted one set of views more than the other:

> Two kinds of purpose are recognised in the report, but their relationship is not made explicit. One kind has to do with the functioning of language in adult life and this is dealt with summarily in seven paragraphs of introduction. The other kind, which is given primary focus, has to do with the functioning of the language in four different aspects of child development in schooling: intellectual, social, personal and aesthetic. It seems to me that a crucial question arises here, namely: how do these purposes relate? How do these different aspects of development nurtured in school actually *prepare* the pupils for the use of language in the adult world? (*ibid.*, p. 78)

Widdowson also indicated that there was a difference in the priority accorded to these two purposes for English depending on whether or not someone was involved in education:

> It is clear from the evidence received by the Committee that people *within* education tend to think of purpose primarily in terms of the development of the child in the process of schooling, whereas those *outside* education tend to think of purpose primarily in terms of adult needs which pupils have to be prepared to meet. (*ibid.*, p. 177)

It is probably true to say that those who believe the main purpose for teaching English in schools to be functional are seldom involved directly in education, but often come into contact with young people at the end of compulsory schooling at 16, for example, in the role of employer, or in post-compulsory education in the role of tutor in further or higher education. A frequently articulated worry is that young people's competence in reading, writing and communication is declining. Alternatively, the argument has taken the form that young people leaving school are not adequately equipped to enter the 'world of work' as it exists in the late twentieth century. The detail of an adequate preparation in literacy and language for adult life, citizenship or the 'world of work' has been rather less easy to identify. While it is easy to specify what appears to be wrong, or lacking, it appears to be much more difficult to articulate a better alternative.

Those within education, particularly teachers, have tended to see the issue in a different way. Although accepting the importance of preparing pupils for their future lives, many teachers, even in the primary sector, would argue that emphasis only on the functional purposes of English is not enough. They would argue that language is a central mode of expressing individuality and social experience, and therefore the subject has a central role in developing the expression of feelings, and the imagination and values of young people. A study of the beliefs and personal priorities of English teachers and student teachers in the UK and USA at secondary level showed that both experienced and student teachers placed the personal/moral/aesthetic development of pupils above specific preparation for adult life and employment (Fox *et al.*, 1993). Schools and teacher education courses have, in recent years, been criticized by government policy-makers and employers' organizations for placing too little emphasis on the functional, or adult-needs, aspects of English, and too much emphasis on English teaching as a means of developing moral/ aesthetic values. However, teachers have often been suspicious of supporting an entirely functional approach to the subject which might appear to be of greater benefit to future employers than to the pupils and students whom they teach. It is also the case that, although a functional, adult-needs emphasis has the appeal of seeming relevant to the lives of young people, it is often a spurious relevance. Teachers, and others, have expressed concern that if there were too strong an emphasis on the adult-needs or employment-relevant aspects, access to some forms of literacy and language might be restricted for pupils who were not academically oriented.

The functional and developmental purposes of English are not mutually exclusive – although, as Widdowson indicated, there has been a lack of clarity about the exact nature of the relationship between a primarily developmental purpose and one which is rather more functional, based on a view of pupils' needs as adults. It is probably also true to say that there are differences in belief about the relative emphasis placed on these perspectives at different times and stages in the education system and, in some cases, for different kinds of pupils. For example, the most obvious purpose of English in the early years of schooling is to enable pupils to read and write, and to initiate them into the educational and wider social uses of literacy. Thus a key purpose for English during this phase is to enable children to function adequately and easily in the world, and to make sense of the environment around them. A further aspect of such a purpose for English is the use of literacy to learn – both inside and outside formal educational settings. Children's initial induction into literacy in the early years is largely the job of the primary school, in partnership with home and the wider community. At this stage, there is a clear functional purpose for English: that all children have the basic knowledge and skills necessary to be able to communicate adequately in school and in the wider world, and to be able to learn in other curriculum subjects.

It is worth noting that in the latter years of the nineteenth century and again in the years immediately after the First World War, the ability of the majority of people to read, understand and enjoy key works of literature in English was thought to be one way in which social cohesion might be generated and maintained. These sentiments had already been articulated by Matthew Arnold, and others, in the nineteenth century. In *Culture and Anarchy* Arnold (1932 [1869]) argued that culture, and particularly literature, could exert a civilizing effect on the new middle classes of industrialized Britain, who might then serve as a model to inspire the proletarian masses and unite different classes in a common culture. After the First World War, these ideas were reiterated in the Newbolt Report (Board of Education, 1921) on the teaching of English, which regarded education, with English at its centre, as having the potential to exert a humanizing and civilizing influence in society. It argued that such a development would also be a source of unity between classes, healing the divide between rich and poor. The arguments put forward by Arnold, and later in the Newbolt Report, were a response to the increasing industrialization and mechanization of society at the time, and to the resulting social changes. They were also a response to the generally held belief that the curriculum of the elementary schools of the late nineteenth and early twentieth centuries should offer a rigidly functional or utilitarian education, in which the children of the working classes were taught little more than basic skills in reading, writing and arithmetic. Arnold's concern was about the wider education of the mass of people who were newly enfranchised by the 1867 Reform Act; the concern of Newbolt was to maintain national unity and establish social cohesion immediately after the First World War.

A minority of people may still believe in a narrowly utilitarian focus in literacy, but there is now general agreement in the developed world that acceptable competence in literacy should extend beyond the basic ability to read and write simple texts. What is much more complex is to identify the full range of purposes for which adults use language and literacy in their lives, and the ways in which these purposes may change over time. Perhaps only once we have begun to do this adequately may we begin to undertake the process of identifying how the developmental purposes of English relate to the needs of individuals living within complex social and cultural networks. As I have already argued, distinctions between those who prioritize the functional adult-needs purposes of English and those who see its primary role as developmental are, in practice, less clearly drawn and polarized. However, the two positions do represent key areas of difference in belief about the primary purpose of the subject.

## The content of English

Over the years, there have been substantial differences of emphasis over the proper content of English. A major division has been between those who regard literature as its academic base, and those who believe that a stronger emphasis should be placed upon language and communication. Priorities relating to the purpose of English have also had an impact on those relating to the content of the subject. For example, if its primary purpose is to prepare young people for adult life, this will influence the content thought to be appropriate and relevant in achieving that aim. A further factor is the particular view taken of pupils' future adult roles: whether they will be expected to fit into the role of acquiescent and unquestioning employees, or whether they are seen as having an active, critical role as citizens. If the former, then the content of English thought to be appropriate is more likely to emphasize correct ways of using language and the learning of rules. If the latter, it is likely that there will be a greater emphasis on understanding how language works as a system; how it is used to communicate meaning; and how it functions in the construction of social reality and in the shaping of opinion. If the primary purpose of English is developmental, this will also have an impact on the content that is thought to be most appropriate, and, again, it will depend on the degree of emphasis within such a perspective. A view of the primary purpose of English as the development of personal aesthetic, moral and spiritual values would most probably place greater emphasis on the study of literary works thought to embody and exemplify such values and qualities.

It is important to bear in mind that there is also a difference between the professional identities of primary school teachers and those in secondary schools which will inform their priorities in relation to the content of the subject. The subject knowledge of most English teachers in secondary schools is primarily literary. The study of literary texts tends to be dominant in the majority of advanced English courses. The systematic study of language belongs to the separate discipline of linguistics. Even where language study does form a part of the degree syllabus in English, it usually takes the form of historical linguistics or philology, based upon analysis of literary texts from the Anglo-Saxon or medieval periods. Most English graduates are, in fact, literature graduates. This phenomenon undoubtedly has influenced the values and subject knowledge of graduates training to be teachers and has informed beliefs about the relative emphasis that should be placed upon language and literature within the school curriculum (Poulson *et al.*, 1996).

Many prospective teachers may themselves have limited knowledge about the formal structure and workings of the English language. This situation has been a source of concern for some time. It was mentioned in the Bullock Report in 1976, which led to the inclusion of a language study element in most, if not all, teacher education courses in England and Wales. It also led to the establishment of the Kingman Committee, in 1987, to investigate the teaching of the English language and, following this, a major national in-service programme for teachers: the Language in the National Curriculum project (LINC).

However, a recent source of dispute about the content of English has been less to do with whether it should consist largely of language or literature than with the *kinds* of language and literature, and the particular emphasis *within* them. The key differences here are between those who believe that literature courses should concentrate on the teaching of a traditional, and relatively unchanging, body of great literature to pupils and university students. This narrowly defined body of work usually includes and emphasizes key texts in the historical development of English literature, such as Beowulf, and the major works of Chaucer, Shakespeare, Milton, Wordsworth, Tennyson. More modern or accessible texts tend to be regarded as inferior. Opposed to this view is one that sees literature as something more flexible and subject to change, and which reflects the tastes and preoccupations of different periods in history.

From this perspective, what is valuable and worth studying changes with time and includes a wide range of novels, plays, poetry and other types of writing. Because English is used widely across the world, the literature studied by pupils may include that written by North Americans, Australians, and African, Caribbean

13

and Chinese writers. For example, Joseph Conrad, generally held to be one of the most important writers of the late nineteenth and early twentieth centuries, wrote in English although it was his third language. In secondary schools and universities, the subject has been influenced by recent developments in literary theory, philosophy and the emerging discipline of cultural studies. These developments gained strength within university English departments in the 1970s and 1980s, and challenged the validity of the traditional university English literature curriculum which emphasized the study of texts by major authors. Similar issues underlie the differences in emphasis in relation to the teaching of English language. This issue will be examined in greater detail in Chapter 5, but in summary they centre on whether there should be direct teaching of traditional grammar, punctuation and other skills, or whether these things should be taught in the context of learning about language in use and in relation to pupils' own reading and writing.

## English and the nature of knowledge

There is another, potentially more complex, dimension to the disputes about English. This is based on beliefs about the nature of knowledge and the best way to transmit or reproduce the knowledge that is accepted as important within a subject or, more generally, within a society. In this respect the key difference tends to be between people who place high value on exclusive cultural traditions and the maintenance of authority and the status quo, and those who value challenge, diversity and change. The former group tend to believe that knowledge is relatively fixed and is best learned in separate subjects, whereas the latter regard it as less fixed and subject to change and reformulation. Values at this level inform those relating to the purpose and content of English, and ways of teaching it. It is perfectly possible for two people to be in accord in their beliefs about the content and purpose of English and yet still be fundamentally opposed, if they hold different beliefs about the nature of knowledge, and the ways in which it should be transmitted or reformulated for succeeding generations.

These fundamental structuring values, and the critical differences between them, are rarely made explicit in debates about education in general, and more specifically in those about English. Such values are frequently invisible to those who hold them, who see their particular world-view as constituting common sense and a position that most reasonable people would support. Problems arise when we are unaware of the deep differences in beliefs and values which underlie the debates about English, about education, and about the workings of wider society. However, if we regard our own values and beliefs as normal, reasonable and common-sense, and fail to recognize that they *are* beliefs and values and part of a continuum of acceptable beliefs within a society at any particular moment, then we may be unable to accept that there are other versions of common sense that hold for people with different beliefs and values. In this instance, it is easy for those who hold different beliefs or ascribe to different values, to be represented as irrational, foolish or dogmatic.

Most recently, a failure to acknowledge such differences in values has been evident in discussions on how to raise educational standards. Frequently, common sense has been equated with tradition, authority and acceptance of fixed bodies of knowledge. Beliefs and values that differ have been pilloried as progressive, or 'trendy'. In the political rhetoric of the 1980s and 1990s, concern for the maintenance of educational standards was set in opposition to what were dismissively labelled as permissive, progressive and trendy teaching methods. Progressive methods were never clearly, or consistently, defined or identified. However, such attacks served as a form of political scaremongering, and precluded the serious consideration of any alternative.

A central feature of this rhetoric was the fear that teachers' attitudes and values were not totally in accord with those of government. The beliefs and values informing the actions of a political party in government were claimed as synonymous with views held by the majority of parents with children in state-maintained schools. The relationship between parents and schools increasingly has been expressed in the language of market forces or industrial production, where education is the commodity, schools the producers, and parents the consumers. Whether the terminology and structures of commodity and service production

15

are appropriate to education has not been questioned. However, both research (e.g. Hughes *et al.*, 1994) and recent events in schools have shown that parents do not necessarily share the values and priorities of government ministers in the education of their children.

In summary, the recent disputes about English centred on a failure to acknowledge that there were substantial differences in emphasis in the beliefs and values informing ideas about the form it ought to take in the school curriculum. This failure led to conflict between teachers (supported by parents and school governors) and politicians, over the curriculum content and assessment of English. None of these beliefs and values was entirely wrong or right; all came from deeply held, but different, sets of beliefs and values. However, it is only when the two different possible polarities are accepted as such that dispute and disagreement can begin to be resolved. An important factor in identifying the source of such differences is an understanding of the way in which English came to hold such an important place in the school curriculum, and the ideas and arguments that informed the development of the subject.

# 2

# The development of English as a subject in the school curriculum

## English and the idea of a liberal education

The differences in attitudes, beliefs and values which have underpinned recent debates about English did not emerge only as a consequence of developments in the school curriculum from the mid-1980s; they have existed for much longer, although they may not have been articulated so explicitly. This chapter examines how and why these different ways of thinking about English as a school subject developed over time. Although English has been accepted as the primary language in England since the fourteenth century, the status of vernacular literature was less clear for a long time. English literature, including the works now regarded as classic literary texts, has not always enjoyed the privileged status that it enjoys today. Indeed, English did not become a recognized subject in the school or university curriculum until the final decades of the nineteenth century and the first two of the twentieth century. Its emergence as a distinct subject reflects the interplay of differences of opinion about its primary purpose in the education system and differing ideas as to what should constitute its proper content and how it should be taught.

A major factor in the development of English as a distinct subject was the expansion of educational provision, particularly the development of a system of maintained schools. The Forster Education Act of 1870 made provision to fill gaps in the existing system of grants to voluntary societies to run schools for the children of the lower orders of society. Its aim was to provide a cheap and basic education concentrating on the rudiments of reading, writing and arithmetic – the traditional three Rs – and some other skills of practical relevance. It is no coincidence that the 1870 Education Act followed fast behind the extension of the franchise in 1867, which included lower-middle- and working-class men in the electorate. There was concern, particularly among the traditional ruling classes, that democratic rights had been extended to people who were relatively uneducated. It is also arguable that changing conditions of economic production in Britain meant that there was a need for a workforce which was minimally literate and numerate. In 1867, Robert Lowe informed the House of Commons that he believed it would be necessary for the newly enfranchised population to be at least literate (Mathieson, 1975, p. 30). Lowe recommended that English should have a place in the elementary schools because he believed it to be a useful subject which offered preparation for life, unlike Classics, which he regarded as being of little use to the lower orders of society. Thus a key aim of the publicly funded elementary schools, established under the direction of local School Boards, was to teach the functional skills of reading and writing. The curricula of the early elementary schools, and of the private schools outside the control of the established Church, had a strong emphasis on utilitarian values: they prioritized useful knowledge which would befit the pupils' future role in life and social standing.

Educational provision for the upper and middle classes in Britain in the nineteenth century was made through the system of public and endowed schools, most of which had a curriculum based entirely on the classical languages, then considered to be the foundation of a humanistic and liberal education. Both Latin and Greek were also necessary for entry into Oxford and Cambridge. In the early years of the nineteenth century, there was considerable discussion and debate, particularly among the middle classes, about the dominance of Classics in the school curriculum. Late-eighteenth- and early-nineteenth-century radicals, such as the Edgeworth family, were keen to see education reformed. They argued that far from providing a liberal and humanistic education, the study of Greek and Latin in public and grammar schools usually entailed rote learning and memorizing language forms by heart, and that pupils rarely engaged with works of philosophy or literature.

Reform of some of the major public schools had in fact been undertaken by men such as Thomas Arnold at Rugby. A new ethos was established which emphasized manly Christian virtues and in which Greek and Roman literature, philosophy and history were considered to be a humanizing and civilizing influence. Such reforms notwithstanding, the Clarendon Commission, which investigated public schools in the mid-nineteenth century, had reported that teaching of Latin and Greek was often done badly, with pupils gaining little of worth from the study of Latin and Greek literature. In spite of the findings and recommendations of the commission, and in the face of increasing arguments for the importance of science and technology in the school curriculum, there was still strong opposition within the public schools to any change from the classics as the basis of the curriculum. The arguments put forward in defence of the classical curriculum insisted that the study of Greek and Latin afforded access to the wisdom and learning of the ancient civilizations (Mathieson, 1975, p. 22). A classical education was also regarded as the hallmark of a gentleman.

English did not figure in the curricula of the major public and endowed schools for boys; at best it was thought that they might amuse themselves with works of English literature as recreation. It was regarded as a subject more suitable for women. Indeed, it was studied by many women in the early years of its inclusion in the university curriculum. It was also popular with both women and men as a subject within the widespread university extension movement in the late nineteenth century. Although a classical education was considered inappropriate and unsuitable for the lower classes and for women of all classes, the notion of a liberal education, whether in Classics or in modern languages, was promoted in the nineteenth century. Education that had utility as its basis was seen as dangerous by many, particularly in an age where the traditional authority of the Church and religion had begun to disintegrate as the population moved away from rural communities into the expanded manufacturing and industrial towns and cities. This perspective had much support from the upper classes, who were resistant to the power and influence of an industrial and commercial society.

There was considerable concern that an elementary education which was entirely utilitarian would not provide any moral or spiritual training for pupils. English literature and culture were identified by people of influence, such as Arnold, as a means of providing an accessible civilizing and humanizing influence for the middle and working classes, just as Classics did for the upper classes. The Newcastle Commission of 1861, investigating education in elementary schools, had also recommended that pupil teachers should study English language and literature, just as Greek and Latin were studied in the public schools. Underlying Arnold's promotion of English as a morally and spiritually educative subject was a concern about the increasingly mechanized society and materialistic values of nineteenth-century Britain. He, and others, believed that a utilitarian, elementary education, teaching basic literacy but without any guiding sense of moral and aesthetic discrimination, would merely reflect the predominantly materialist values of a mechanized industrial society:

> The great fault of the instruction in our elementary schools is that it at most gives to a child the mechanical possession of the instruments of knowledge, but does nothing to form him, to put him in the way of making the best possible use of them. (Board of Education, 1908, p. 178)

Arnold believed that such a basic form of education would not protect the mass of people from the influence of popular literature, magazines and newspapers, which had become cheaper and more accessible after the middle of the century. He regarded culture, in the form of classical literature for the upper classes and English poetry and literature for others, as a unifying and redeeming force in Victorian society. In *Culture and Anarchy,* (1932 [1869]) Arnold argued that culture sought to do away with class divisions, making accessible to all the best thought and knowledge available in the world. This, he believed, would help 'to make all men live in an atmosphere of sweetness and light' (p. 112).

As an inspector of schools, Matthew Arnold recommended that pupil teachers in elementary schools memorize lines of great poetry in English. His view was that recitation of poetry in class would help to form taste and judgement in pupils. Arnold's promotion of English literature and grammar helped to establish it as a separate 'specific' subject to be taught in the upper years of elementary schools and, in 1882, as a compulsory class subject. Thus, in the latter part of the nineteenth century, the role and status of English were being delineated. Its role in promoting basic literacy among the lower orders was obvious, and this aspect of the subject was regarded by some as its chief function in the school curriculum. In addition, and sometimes in opposition, there were those who believed that English should have a wider role in education – that it should also serve social and moral purposes.

At the same time as the nature and role of English in the elementary school curriculum and its relationship to Classics were being defined, a number of key British cultural institutions and landmarks were established: for example, in the 1850s entry to the Civil Service was opened to competitive examination in which English was a central part; the *Oxford English Dictionary* was started in 1884; the *Dictionary of National Biography* in 1885; and the National Trust in 1895. Each of these contributed to the identification and establishment of a clear concept of nationhood and national pride which coincided with increasing British colonial expansion, particularly in India and Africa. During the nineteenth century, there was a move to establish a greater degree of political control in India. Along with this went cultural control. In 1835 Macaulay had argued for an education system in India that included culture and literature in English: 'Wherever British literature spreads, may it be attended by British virtue and British freedom' (Trevelyan, 1900, pp. 290–2). Thus English as a language and as literature had an important role in consolidating and promoting the identity of Britain as a colonial power – not only politically but also culturally. The notion of English as a world language, which will be discussed more fully in the final chapter, also began to emerge at this time. Nationhood, cast as 'Englishness', was closely linked to discourses about the language (Crowley, 1989). By the end of the nineteenth century, English had begun to be recognized as a subject worthy of study in its own right, rather than as a useful basic skill to be taught in elementary schools. The work of individuals such as Arnold did much to establish a broader concept of English within the elementary school curriculum; and the establishment of a system of secondary schools after 1902 also helped to secure its existence. Others involved in the extension of university courses emphasized the importance of literature in a wider concept of education. However, English was still far from having a clearly recognized and accepted status and disciplinary structure.

## The Newbolt Committee: a secure place for English in the school curriculum

The early decades of the twentieth century saw the nature and role of English established more firmly in both school and university curricula. One of the important ways in which this was achieved was through the establishment of the English Association in 1906, which was to have an important influence in promoting English – in defining its content as a subject, and in debating the most appropriate ways in which it should be taught (Ball, 1983). One of the early tasks of the association was to draw together the separate strands of grammar, composition and recitation/literature and to unify these into a distinct subject. The association's increasing influence is reflected in a 1910 Board of Education Circular on the teaching of English in secondary schools, in which a committee of members of the English Association had a consultative and advisory role. The membership of the association, particularly of the committees that advised the Board of Education, was very much associated with the Establishment, despite the apparently radical nature of its proposals with regard to the teaching of English language. The circular acknowledged that English had a clear role in education beyond the elementary schools. Echoing an earlier Board of Education document, the 1905 *Suggestions for Consideration of Teachers*, it also challenged the use of the traditional grammatical and philological methods of classics teaching as a basis for the study of English, stating that this was based on a set of misconceptions about the nature of grammar. Instead of the parsing and analysis of sentence structure, the teaching of grammar was seen as best taught in relation to literature and in connection with developing the skills of written composition:

Grammar should not bulk largely in the regular school teaching of
English, and it should not be isolated from composition and literature
and made into an abstract exercise. Whole lesson periods should not
be systematically given up to formal grammar (Board of Education,
1910, p. 11)

The document also echoed some of the newer ways of
understanding the nature of learning and the conceptualization
of human development. Ideas about child development, such as
those of Rousseau and, later, Froebel, were influential in
educational thinking in the late nineteenth and early twentieth
centuries. Particularly important for English was the recognition of
a connection between individual development and self-expression.
An influential metaphor in discourses about child development and
education was one of organic growth that needed careful
nurturing. Froebel's work emphasized the importance of spon-
taneous activity, the value of sensory experience, the involvement
of children in the learning process, and provision of the right sort
of environment for pupils to thrive. The ideas of the American
educational philosopher John Dewey were also introduced into
Britain in the 1890s through the British Association of Child
Study (Mathieson, 1975). In particular, his theories of how
children were motivated, and the importance of direct experience,
were influential, at least at the level of the Schools' Inspectorate
and Board of Education. The idea of the child as a developing
person had begun to displace that of the child as an empty vessel,
waiting to filled. Rigid rote learning and memorization had been
the predominant approach to teaching in the mid- and late-
Victorian elementary schools, although it had been criticized by
educators as early as the mid-nineteenth century.

Edmund Holmes in 1911 described how, in the early phase of
elementary education, the emphasis had been firmly on trans-
mission of knowledge, rather than on encouraging self-expression:

self-expression on the part of the child may be said to have been
formally prohibited by all who were responsible for the elementary
education of the children of England, and also to have been prohibited
de facto by all the unformulated conditions under which the
elementary school was conducted. (Holmes, 1911, p. 155)

However, self-expression in the education of children in elementary schools in the early twentieth century tended to mean that pupils composed essays on a topic related to their personal experience, as opposed to copying a written composition. It did not necessarily involve anything less structured or radical in modern-day terms.

I have already argued that issues in the teaching of English, and the nature and role of the subject within the school curriculum, do not occur in isolation from larger social, political and cultural developments. This is nowhere more evident than in one of the key documents in the development of English as a central subject in the school curriculum in this century: the report of the Newbolt Committee, published in 1921. Although the English Association was strongly represented in the membership of the committee, its report was very much a reflection of the prevailing mood of the period in which it was written. At the end of the First World War, there was a widespread concern in Britain to improve social conditions, particularly educational provision, not least because conscription had revealed British soldiers to be poorly educated in comparison to their German counterparts. While echoes of the arguments of Matthew Arnold can be detected in the text of the Newbolt Report, the predominant tone was patriotic: it sought to promote unity between classes within a wider conception of nationhood, and it identified a key role for English language and literature in helping to establish this. The report made a strong case for English language and literature as a central subject of the curriculum in both elementary and secondary schools. English, it was argued, would provide a unifying focus for the nation after the war. The study of English literature would encourage a sense of national pride and national identity which had the possibility of unifying the discord between classes:

> The English people might learn as a whole to regard their own language, first with respect, and then with a genuine feeling of pride and affection. More than any mere symbol, it is actually a part of England: to maltreat it or deliberately debase it would be seen to be an outrage; to become sensible of its significance and splendour would be to step upon a higher level ... Such a feeling for our own native language would be a bond of union between all classes and would

beget the right kind of national pride. Even more certainly should pride and joy in the national literature serve as such a bond. This feeling, if fostered in all our schools without exception, would disclose itself far more often and furnish a common meeting ground for great numbers of men and women who might otherwise have never come into touch with one another. (Board of Education, 1921, pp. 22–3)

The Newbolt Report made strong claims for the role of English in national renewal and education. With an even stronger emphasis, it adopted arguments similar to those of Arnold and his contemporaries in promoting the importance of literature in moral education. It also promoted the idea that the study of literature should form a central part of the understanding of a British – or rather English – cultural heritage. However, it is important to note that the concept of a national language, even in the early years of the twentieth century, was still being contested. Many people concerned with either education or language indicated the extent to which the people in Britain were divided not only by differences in status and wealth, but also by differences in language. Language was one of the strongest markers of social class. Around the turn of the last century, there was still considerable diversity in spoken language, and many dialect forms were used on a daily basis by the lower classes. Indicated in the writing of the period is an awareness of a gradual shift towards a more standardized spoken language. The Newbolt Report acknowledged the divided nature of British society of the period and the important role that language played in dividing or uniting classes:

> Two causes, both accidental and conventional rather than national, at present distinguish and divide one class from another in England. The first of these is a marked difference in their modes of speech. If the teaching of the language were properly and universally provided for, the difference between educated and uneducated speech, which at present causes so much prejudice and difficulty of intercourse on both sides, would gradually disappear. (*ibid.*, pp. 21–2)

However, before such a situation was guaranteed, the Newbolt Committee maintained that standard English would need to be established by being taught in the elementary schools:

Plainly, then, it is the first and chief duty of the Elementary Schools to give its pupils speech – to make them articulate and civilised human beings, able to communicate themselves in speech and writing, and be able to receive the communication of others.... Indeed, until they have been given civilised speech it is useless to talk of continuing their education, for, in a real sense, their education has not been begun. (*ibid.*, p. 60).

Thus one of the key functions of teaching English was to ensure that standard English was taught and learned in schools, and that 'uncivilized' usage or 'barbarisms' were eradicated in the speech of working-class children. The report had little attachment to linguistic diversity: it regarded many children as coming from homes that were linguistically deficient. 'The great difficulty of teachers in elementary schools in many districts is that they have to fight against the powerful influences of evil habits of speech contracted in the home and street.' (*ibid.*, p. 59).

## English and national unity after the First World War

Thus, there was a difference between the argument for the teaching of English in elementary schools in order to ensure that the population had the basic ability to read and write, and the claim made in the Newbolt Report, and by such people as Sampson (1926), that a further role for English was the training of children to speak a standardized form of language, with the intention of eradicating differences of class and social status. The role of standard English in promoting a concept of nationhood and national identity will be discussed in Chapter 5. However, a key aspect of the Newbolt Report was the notion that English language, as well as literature, could be used as a cultivating and humanizing influence. It is worth emphasizing that not only were an appreciation of literature and good language use seen as helpful in establishing a sense of national pride and unity, but also they were seen as influences that would help to counteract the materialism and mechanism of an industrial and increasingly modern society. Just as Arnold and others had expressed concern about the materialism in society brought about by industrialization and the expansion of trade in the nineteenth century, there was an even greater concern in the early decades of the twentieth century that society was becoming more fragmented. The way of conceptualizing English as a subject which provided a source of moral, aesthetic sustenance against the demands of a mechanized, dehumanized world was already being established at the time of the Newbolt Committee.

While government commissions and committees of inquiry, such as that chaired by Henry Newbolt, might reflect contemporary thinking on the nature and purpose of the English curriculum in schools, it is less easy to ascertain the extent to which this reflected what was happening in practice, or the degree to which the committee's recommendations affected practice. It has been argued that in many respects the liberal recommendations of the report did not substantially affect practice in schools. The kinds of teaching methods and approaches that were discussed were often developed in particular contexts and by charismatic and confident individuals, such as the work undertaken by Caldwell Cook at the Perse School in Cambridge. For example, in 1918, at an English Association conference, F. S. Boas, a member of the committee and Vice-President of the English Association, argued strongly against a narrow and limited form of English for pupils in elementary schools. While acknowledging that there should be different types of work in English for pupils in different schools, he suggested none the less that there should be a balance of content and that literature should be a prominent feature of the English curriculum for all children (Ball, 1985).

However, it is not adequate to dismiss as unrepresentative of common practice the developments described in the Newbolt Report, nor to dismiss the approaches recommended therein as being taken up only by a small minority of teachers and schools. While establishing the centrality of literature within the English curriculum and its important role in fostering a common national identity, cutting across class divisions, the report also acknowledged that the study of literature had the potential to be used to promote personal development and creativity. The work of such educators as Caldwell Cook was highlighted. The role of English, particularly of literature, in stimulating discussion, debate and drama, was also identified in the Hadow Report (Board of

Education, 1926), which discussed the purpose of different phases of education within the elementary system. Hadow acknowledged the need to reconcile the destiny of the elementary school child, who was likely to enter employment at the age of 14, with the notion of a liberal, self-enhancing education. The Hadow Report moves clearly beyond recommending the study of great works of literature because they are part of a national heritage, or because they would be morally and aesthetically educational, towards a position of seeing literature as having a wider role in developing creativity and self-expression. Similarly, the function of English language as a means of encouraging individual personal expression, rather than merely the learning of a set of rules for the correct use of the language, was being identified at this time.

The two key concepts in discussions about education and society in the years after the First World War were the importance of the individual and the potential of education to nurture and value individual expression and creativity. These developed from a strong desire for a better world and a more peaceable and just society after the sacrifices of the war. In *Education: Its Data and First Principles* (1920), Percy Nunn made a strong case for the importance of encouraging individuality, personal uniqueness and the child's potential for creativity. He argued that the one of the failings of education was that it had neglected the development of feelings. An education system that acknowledged the importance of the affective dimension of human life was, he suggested, the way to progress as a society.

Throughout the inter-war and post-1945 years, there was an increasing emphasis on the importance of the affective dimensions of education, and on the potential that English had to contribute to these. The education of the emotions and the development of fine discrimination would, it was believed, help to create a different sort of citizen, one who would not make the mistakes of the past. The idealism of progressive views of education was related in some respects to those which were less progressive, but which shared a belief in the importance of the affective aspects of education, and the nurturing of fine discrimination and taste, particularly against the spread of mass culture and leisure. Developments in industry, transport and leisure activity served to emphasize this concern, and it is echoed in many of the documents and in the literature of the inter-war period, for example, in Eliot's poetry and in the major novels of D. H. Lawrence. In particular, there was a deep suspicion towards the increasing influence of the mass media, such as newspapers, magazines and cheap books, and the cinema, particularly in the lives of working-class people. There was also a considerable degree of sentimental nostalgia for the passing of what were regarded as the traditional rural communities and occupations of England, their cultural traditions and social relationships. This nostalgic view represented pre-industrialized Britain – or rather England – as being made up of self-sufficient organic communities with authentic lifestyles and social relationships. In contrast, modern urban life was regarded as spiritually impoverished, culturally barren and socially fragmented.

The notion of English, particularly English literature, as providing moral ammunition against an increasingly materialistic world was a powerful influence on developments in the subject. English at Cambridge and other universities in the 1920s and 1930s, under individuals such as Quiller-Couch, Richards and later Leavis, was influential in establishing the centrality of the study of literature within the subject. From the 1930s until the 1970s, Leavis had a substantial influence on thinking about the purpose and content of English in universities, in university education departments responsible for training English teachers, and eventually in secondary schools. At the centre of the Leavisite endeavour was a belief in the importance of the study of literature and its central role in personal, moral and aesthetic development, which would serve as a barrier to the encroachment of mass forms of entertainment.

In the period 1870–1939, some of the central tenets of debates and conflicts about the purpose, content and most appropriate way of teaching and learning English were shaped. In the latter years of the nineteenth century, there was a growing awareness that schools needed to do more than provide the basics of reading and writing, and should be aiming to promote an appreciation of English literature and language. At that time, there was also a recognition of the role of British – or, more accurately, English – literature in promoting a distinct national identity. This notion was

29

promoted as much abroad, and especially in colonized territories, as in the British Isles. Within Britain, arguments for the civilizing and tempering role of literature focused on its potential to help resist the values of urban society, mass culture, and the other effects of an industrial and market economy. After the First World War, importance began to be attributed to the affective dimension of education, and to individual development. In this area, the encouragement of personal response in English, along with drama and art, had great importance. This period also saw the gradual establishment of English as a distinct subject within the secondary school and university curricula, and its broadening in the elementary schools to include an aspect of the expressive use of language and the study of literature. To understand the underlying arguments which have surfaced in more recent years, it is illuminative to examine these issues within a longer time span, and to identify the connections between earlier developments in relation to the subject and the arguments that are being aired in present times. The following chapters examine how some of the issues which arose in connection with establishing English as an important school subject were echoed again in contemporary debates and disputes about English in the school curriculum, particularly in relation to the 1988 Education Reform Act and the National Curriculum.

# 3

# Towards a national curriculum

## The uncertainties of the 1970s and 1980s

In the period after the 1944 Education Act, English had an established and secure place in the new primary and secondary school system, and it might be thought that there was little cause for further discussion of the issues. However, that proved not to be the case: the debate about English re-emerged from the late 1960s onwards, and began to attract more and more attention from the late 1970s onwards. It was to become one of the most strongly contested issues in the imposition of a centralized national curriculum, in which it was one of the compulsory core subjects. The National Curriculum involved radical change imposed by central government, without the involvement of schools or teachers. Long before the Education Reform Act of 1988, there had been concern about the direction which English, and education in general, was taking.

A research study conducted by Start and Wells (1972) for the National Foundation for Educational Research indicated that reading standards were lower for children from poorer families than for those of children from more prosperous ones. The study prompted debate and concern about standards of literacy in schools, because even if there was no clear evidence that standards were falling, there was a feeling that despite the investment in education since 1945, standards of literacy did not appear to have improved. The then Secretary of State for Education, Margaret Thatcher, set up a committee of inquiry chaired by Sir Alan Bullock to investigate standards of literacy and the teaching of English.

The terms of reference of the committee were

> to consider in relation to schools: (a) all aspects of teaching the use of English, including reading, writing, and speech; (b) how present practice might be improved and the role that initial and in-service training might play; (c) to what extent arrangements for monitoring the general level of attainment in these skills can be introduced or improved; and to make recommendations. (DES, 1975, p. xxxi)

The report of this committee, entitled *A Language for Life* (DES, 1975), but more commonly known as the Bullock Report, presented a comprehensive and detailed examination of practice in the teaching of English in primary and secondary schools. It measured claims about reading standards against available evidence and it gave careful consideration to the role of language in pupils' learning. The report began by identifying the anxieties about English and the teaching of literacy outlined above, indicating that at times of such anxiety

> there is likely to be a wistful look back at the past, with a conviction, often illusory, that times were better then than now. And the times that people claim to have been better are generally within the span of their own lives. (*ibid.*, p. 3)

The first chapter of the Bullock Report indicated that many of the allegations of lower standards came from employers, who maintained that young people starting work could not write grammatically, were poor spellers, and expressed themselves badly in language. It also pointed out that the Newbolt Report of 1921 documented similar observations at the end of the First World War.

In the discussion of attitudes to English, three approaches were outlined. These related, in some respects, to the differences in belief about its nature and purpose identified in Chapter 1 of this book. The first approach identified by Bullock is one in which English is seen as an instrument of personal moral or aesthetic growth; the second gives priority to the teaching of skills in reading and writing; a third is identified as being concerned with English as vehicle for social change. However, the text of *A Language for Life* stresses that none of these views of the subject dominated in the evidence collected in the survey, contrary to generalizations being made in the media and elsewhere. The report identified some of the issues discussed in Chapter 1 of this book, and, in particular, the complex nature of identifying the content of English with precision:

> It is a characteristic of English that it does not hold together as a body of knowledge which can be identified, quantified then transmitted.... There are two possible responses for the teacher of English, at whatever level. One is to attempt to draw in the boundaries, to impose shape on what seems amorphous, rigour on what seems undisciplined. The other is to regard English as process not content and see the all-inclusiveness as an opportunity rather than a handicap. The first response can lead to a concept of the subject as divisible into compartments, each of which answers to certain formal requirements.... The second response can lead to a readiness to exploit the subject's vagueness of definition, to let it flow where the child's interest will take it. Its exponents feel that the complex of activities that go to make up English cannot be circumscribed and still less quantified; the variables are too numerous and the objects too subtle. (*ibid.*, p. 5)

Information provided by schools suggested that a good deal of time was still allocated to formal practice in English:

> The answers we received did not reveal a picture of decay of such work in the midst of a climate of unchecked creativity.... Our survey gives no evidence of a large body of teachers committed to the rejection of basic skills and not caring who knows it. (*ibid.*, p. 6)

Evidence gathered by the committee of inquiry corroborated neither beliefs about declining standards in literacy, nor beliefs about the spread of permissive approaches to the teaching of English. One of its most important features was the discussion of the complexity of English as a subject and the identification of differing beliefs and values about its proper content, its function and the ways in which it should be taught.

The Bullock Report identified the development of pupils' linguistic capacities as the key purpose for English in schools. It argued that language was an important dimension of the development of human thought and therefore it had a central role in pupils' learning in all areas of the school curriculum. Thus language learning was seen as crucial; however, the report did not support a narrow definition of language learning as a body of static knowledge, or the rules of grammar. Instead, it acknowledged language as a dynamic and changing phenomenon:

> It [referring to the term 'basic skills'] is often read to mean that language abilities can somehow be extracted from context, taught in the abstract, and fed back in. The evidence is that one acquires language as a pattern, not as an inert collection of units added serially, a mechanical accumulation of abstracted parts of speech. (*ibid.*, p. 7)

The report presents a very clear view of the nature of learning and its relationship to knowledge. It argues that a popularly held belief is that knowledge exists independently of the knower; and that the educational debate had been confused by the 'simplistic notion that "being told" is the polar opposite of "finding out for oneself"' (*ibid.*, p. 50). It argues that, rather than existing independently of a knower and being capable of being transmitted by 'being told', knowledge is something that is interpreted within the framework of past knowledge and experience.

A powerful theoretical justification for the centrality of language in all aspects of learning and, indeed, human development was offered in Bullock. It emphasized the schools' role in developing pupils' communicative competence, and the importance of extending awareness of language issues across the whole curriculum. The notion of language across the curriculum, for which the Bullock Report became so well known, had actually originated in a series of conferences and study groups held between 1966 and 1968 which had culminated in a conference at the Institute of Education, organized by the London Association for the Teaching of English. James Britton described one of the principal outcomes of this network as practical: the attempt to persuade staff in schools to get together and work out common policies for language across the whole curriculum (Britton, 1973).

The Bullock Report was certainly influential, particularly in promoting the idea that language had a central place in learning, and that all teachers bore responsibility for the linguistic and communicative competence of their pupils. It also generated awareness of the need for teachers' professional development in this area. It is less easy to ascertain its success in changing schools' practice, as opposed to their policies. Because it had not endorsed simple solutions to perceived falling standards, pointing out that comparisons between standards at different periods of time and different circumstances are often dubious, the report did little to support the cause of those who wished for a return to a mythical golden age in schools, when children could spell and punctuate and express themselves clearly, and when formal analysis of grammar had a secure place in the school curriculum. One of its most important features was that it highlighted the complexity of the language issue and the range of beliefs which people held about the way it should be learned in schools. Furthermore, it stated unequivocally that the debate about the teaching of English language had been confused by views which represented it as the mechanical accumulation of grammatical rules, in the abstract, extracted from context.

## Defining a core curriculum in English from 5 to 16

The Bullock Report had emphasized the role of teachers in all subject areas in promoting literacy and extending pupils' linguistic and communicative competence. However, concern about pupils' knowledge and understanding of the forms and functions of the English language still remained. It increasingly became the subject of government attention after the general election of 1979 had returned a Conservative government, led by Margaret Thatcher. Previously, decisions about what should be taught in the school curriculum were the responsibility of local education authorities and, to a certain extent, individual schools. Starting in 1984, however, a series of documents was published by HMI under the common title of *Curriculum Matters* (DES, 1984). The first volume in the series dealt with English. It was a key document in the movement towards a national curriculum, in that it attempted to clarify the aims and principles of the subject rather than offer or promote any new approach. *Curriculum Matters 1* attempted to define aims and objectives for an English curriculum for pupils from 5 to 16. In doing so, it addressed a key issue: pupils' progression from the early years to the end of compulsory schooling. In particular, it attempted to outline a curriculum that spanned both primary and secondary phases. The curriculum aims included the development of speaking, reading and writing. A fourth aim was identified as teaching pupils about language – one of the earliest formulations of the term 'knowledge about language', later developed in the Kingman and Cox Reports and in the Language in the National Curriculum project, funded by the DES between 1989 and 1992. *Curriculum Matters 1: English 5–16* makes an explicit statement about the teaching of language to pupils,

> so that they achieve working knowledge of its structure and of the variety of ways in which meaning is made, so that they have a vocabulary for discussing it, so that they can use it with greater awareness, and because it is interesting. (*ibid.* p. 3 para. 1.6)

The pamphlet acknowledged that this fourth aim would be contentious: it stated, 'It is likely that there will be little disagreement about these broad aims, with the possible exception of the last' (*ibid.* p. 3, para. 1.7). However, as Bullock had before, it emphasized that this fourth aim of teaching about language should not be decontextualized from language use:

> Learning *about* language is necessary as a means to increasing one's ability to use and respond to it; it is not an end in itself. It should arise from the activities of talking, listening, writing and reading for real purposes; and take the form of encouraging children's curiosity about language. (*ibid.*, p. 14, para. 3.7)

*English 5–16* makes clear that although teaching of grammar exercises might be considered educationally unsound and ineffective as a means of improving pupils' ability to use language, this did not imply that explicit teaching about language should be avoided or ignored. Any such assumptions were challenged strongly:

> There is much confusion over whether grammar should be explicitly taught. It has long been recognised that formal exercises in the analysis and classification of language contribute little or nothing to

the ability to use it. One consequence of this, however, is that many pupils are taught nothing at all about how language works as a system, and consequently do not understand the nature of their mistakes or how to put them right. We suggest that if some attention is given to the examination and discussion of the structure of the language that pupils speak, write, read, or listen to for real purposes, their awareness of its possibilities and pitfalls can be sharpened'. (*ibid.*, p. 14, para. 3.8)

Perhaps even more radical than the support for consistent and systematic teaching of language within the English curriculum was the attempt to specify levels of attainment for pupils at ages 7, 11 and 16, and some means by which progress could be assessed. This specification was crucial to the task of identifying a sequence of progression for all pupils.

Although emphasizing the need for English to include something on the structure of language and its workings as a system, *English 5–16* did not advocate narrow or rigid teaching; nor did it support an entirely functional view of literacy. In the section that discusses principles of English teaching, the document states that 'Good teaching of English, at any level, is far more than the inculcation of skills: it is an education of the intellect and sensibility' (*ibid.*, p. 13, para. 3.2). Although it attempted to set down broad principles for the teaching and assessment of English, while simultaneously addressing many of the concerns about falling standards of literacy and lack of accountability in the curriculum, *English 5–16* was greeted with suspicion on publication and was the object of considerable criticism by those involved in the subject. The National Association for the Teaching of English (NATE) expressed concern at its implications for the future direction of English teaching in schools. Underlying the hostility to *English 5–16*'s attempt to specify curriculum content and levels of attainment for pupils of different ages was a concern that it was part of a larger attack on the autonomy and professional standing of teachers and schools. It was felt that the Department of Education and Science was likely to intervene in such a way as to promote a more rigid and traditional curriculum in schools.

In a second pamphlet, published in 1986, entitled *English 5–16: The Responses to Curriculum Matters 1* (DES, 1986), HMI reported that in response to the original proposals, there was little consensus on the teaching of language, nor any clear trends, other than a widespread and vigorous rejection of grammatical analysis, and 'some growing willingness to settle an agenda and ultimately a curriculum for this aim' (p. 16). The document also pointed out that it would take time for there to be the professional unity required to implement a policy. It recommended a committee of inquiry to focus attention on the matter. The intention was that this would assist the growth of stronger accord among those involved in English teaching, and that it would, ultimately, make recommendations on what should be taught to those intending to become teachers, teachers in post, and pupils in schools. It was largely in response to this recommendation that in early 1987 the Secretary of State for Education, Kenneth Baker, announced the setting up of a committee of inquiry to be chaired by Sir John Kingman; its terms of reference were to make recommendations about the teaching of English language which would inform statutory curriculum policy:

> I am working towards national agreement on the aims and objectives of English teaching in schools in order to improve standards. But I am struck by a particular gap. Pupils need to know the workings of the language if they are to use it effectively. Most schools no longer teach old-fashioned grammar. But little has been put in its place. (Kenneth Baker, press release, 16.1.87)

The composition of the Kingman Committee offered little cause for optimism on the part of English teachers. There were no representatives from the subject association, NATE, nor were there any of the figures such as James Britton, Douglas Barnes, Harold Rosen and Andrew Wilkinson who had had a significant influence on research and teaching in English and language development in the previous two decades. The committee ultimately recommended a model of English language consisting of four parts: the forms of the language; communication and comprehension; the acquisition and development of language; and historical and geographical variation in English.

The Kingman Report elicited little enthusiasm from any quarter. It failed to satisfy critics of what were seen as sloppy, imprecise approaches to the teaching of English language, who had hoped for a recommendation to return to the teaching of formal grammar. Equally, it failed to engage the support of the English teaching profession, as it seemed so remote from the realities of English teaching in 1988. Lack of enthusiasm for the report was summed up in an editorial in the autumn 1988 issue of *English in Education,* which predicted that in years to come, the Kingman Report was unlikely to be regarded as a benchmark in the teaching of English.

## The role of the Cox Committee

The task of formulating a curriculum for English in all its aspects, and levels of attainment to be reached by all children at the ages of 7, 11, 14 and 16, in accordance with the model of assessment formulated by the Task Group on Assessment and Testing, was given to a working group chaired by Professor Brian Cox. Previously, Cox had edited the Black Paper series, and had been a member of the Kingman Committee. The National Curriculum working group contained no representation from the professional association, NATE. When it was established there were few reasons for optimism in English teaching: Brian Cox was closely identified with the radical conservatism of the Black Papers, and it seemed likely that the new curriculum would represent a traditional view of English as a school subject. In the event, the proposals for a National Curriculum included a more balanced view of the subject than had been expected. Both the interim and final reports presented what seemed to be a position of consensus – one in which differences were identified, but could coexist within the same framework. In order to maintain this consensus, difference and dissent had to be minimized. Indeed, the Cox Report made clear that dissent and debate about the nature of the subject and its pedagogies were not necessarily desirable, arguing that

> an unfortunate feature of much discussion of English teaching is the false and unhelpful polarization of views ... people set in opposition to each other's individual or social aims or utilitarian and imaginative

aims, or language and literature ... the best practice reflects a consensus rather than extreme positions. It is important that this is not seen as some timid compromise but rather an attempt to show the relation between these views within a larger framework. (DES, 1989a, p. 2, para. 6)

While there was some critical debate about the initial National Curriculum proposals in general and, more specifically, the proposals for English (e.g. Mathieson, 1991; Crombie and Poulson, 1991), there was little opposition to the outcome of the Cox Committee. The report of the working group was, in general, seen as unobjectionable by most English teachers and academics. Indeed, editorials in the summer 1989 and summer 1990 editions of *English in Education*, following the publication of the Cox Report, suggested a reasonable level of satisfaction with the recommendations of the working group. A survey of those regarded as having an influential role in English teaching in the UK was reported in the summer 1989 edition of the journal, which indicated that, with some exceptions, teachers were happy with the recommendations of the Cox Committee. Respondents indicated that they felt that the National Curriculum could have been a lot worse (*English in Education*, 1989, vol. 15. no. 3, p. 1). The following year, an editorial in the journal attempted to explain why, after initial suspicion and scepticism, the recommendations and statutory order for English were acceptable:

The early vociferous opposition to the very idea of national curriculum English has dwindled into an almost unanimous cautious acceptance. In the absence of any readily identifiable alternative, it seemed better to live with what seems, on the surface, reassuringly familiar. (*English in Education*, 1990, vol 16. no. 3, p. 3)

What was it, then, that made the Cox Report so 'reassuringly familiar' and led it to be more acceptable to English teachers than had been the HMI *Curriculum Matters 1: English 5–16*, or the Kingman Report? First of all, the 1988 Education Reform Act had made provision for a statutory curriculum. That such a thing would or could come about was no longer a subject for speculation; it was law. In such circumstances, there were fears as to what such a statutory curriculum would represent, particularly when the working group for English was chaired by someone generally thought to hold very traditional views on the subject. However, in the end, the recommendations made by the working group did not endorse a narrow conceptualization of the subject, nor did they make undue prescription about the teaching of language as part of the English curriculum.

## English for the National Curriculum

A key to the cautious acceptance of the Cox Report, indicated in *English in Education*, was its inclusiveness and the attempt to represent a spectrum of opinion. In the curriculum recommended by the committee, English was not divided into language or literature but, following the structure of *Curriculum Matters: English 5–16*, instead organized programmes of study for three major strands which comprised reading, writing, and speaking and listening. There were other strands that dealt with spelling and handwriting and knowledge about language. The aim was that knowledge about language should be included in the reading, writing, and speaking and listening strands, and that composition and transcription in writing be dealt with separately. This avoided programmes of study that might appear to be emphasizing the transcriptional aspects of writing such as spelling and handwriting at the expense of learning to compose in a range of written forms for a variety of purposes and audiences. It also seemed to avoid the dispute about the teaching of language and the role of grammar.

The inclusiveness of the Cox recommendations also acknowledged the different purposes for English. Within it, five views of the subject were identified. These were described as:

* cultural heritage, in which pupils were led towards 'an appreciation of those works of literature that have been widely regarded as the finest in the language' (DES, 1989a, para. 2:24). A similar position had been articulated in relation to the study of literature in the Kingman Report, which expressed a fear that

> It is possible that a generation of children might grow up deprived of their entitlement – an introduction to the powerful and splendid history of the best that has been thought and said in our language. Too rigid a concern with what is 'relevant' to the lives of young people seems to pose the danger of impoverishing not only the young people but the culture itself. (DES, 1988, p. 11)

- an adult-needs view, which 'focuses on communication outside the school: it emphasises the responsibility of English teachers to prepare children for the language demands of adult life, including the workplace, in a fast-changing world (*ibid.*, para. 2.23);
- personal growth, 'which focuses on the child: it emphasises the relationship between language and learning in the individual child, and the role of literature in developing children's imaginative and aesthetic lives' (*ibid.*, para. 2.21);
- a cross-curricular view, which 'focuses on the school; it emphasizes that all teachers ... have a responsibility to help children with the language demands of different subjects on the school curriculum' (*ibid.*, para. 2.22);
- a cultural analysis view, which 'emphasises the role of English in helping children towards a critical understanding of the world and cultural environment in which they live' (*ibid.*, para. 2.25).

They were not, as illustrated by the text of the report itself, seen as mutually exclusive and might be combined in several ways.

Of the five views outlined above, three had already been described by Dixon (1966) as having been identified in 1965 at the Dartmouth Seminar, funded by the Carnegie Foundation, to enable Anglo-American discussion on the purpose and content of English. The first of these was described as centred on skills and fitted an era when initial literacy was the primary requirement. The second stressed cultural heritage and reflected the need for what was seen as the civilizing and socially unifying aspect of great literature. The third view, which Dixon identified at the time of the Dartmouth Seminar as the current model, was based upon the notion of English as a vehicle for personal growth. I have outlined earlier, in discussion of the Bullock Report, how and why the cross-curricular view originated. Brian Cox (1991) gave his own account of the making of the Cox Report and argued for the inclusion of the cultural analysis position by stating that in the 1970s and 1980s there had been a growing interest in the problems thrown up by new methods of cultural analysis. He pointed out that traditional ways of teaching English had been questioned because they encouraged passivity on the part of pupils, and submission to authority. Secondary schools encouraged pupils to reproduce teachers' notes and ideas, rather than to develop their own points of view. In contrast, an emphasis on cultural analysis encouraged pupils to examine, for themselves, the underlying assumptions in texts they were studying (Cox, 1991, p. 78). It is clear from Cox's description of the cultural analysis view of English that it would encourage pupils to question social and cultural hierarchies, and to challenge given assumptions and opinions.

In many ways, the five views of English presented in the Cox Report reflect aspects of the different ways of thinking about the subject, as discussed in Chapter 1. The adult-needs and personal growth views reflected beliefs about the purpose of English in the curriculum: in the adult-needs view, its relevance to pupils' future adult lives was emphasized, whereas a personal growth view emphasized its developmental potential. To a certain extent, the cross-curricular view accommodated aspects of the adult-needs and personal growth view, although with less emphasis on the aesthetic/moral dimensions of development than on the cognitive aspects. The cross-curricular view also encompassed beliefs about the content of English – in which learning about language and its uses was the priority, rather than literature. The cultural heritage view reflected a belief that the content of the subject was primarily literary. This view also tended to represent the values of tradition and authority.

The fifth, cultural analysis, view offered a more radical purpose for English, emphasizing the importance of pupils' learning to be critical. This was also primarily developmental in purpose, with underpinning radical beliefs about the nature of knowledge and learning. In many respects, this view of English was largely related to a belief that the most appropriate content was literary – although a much wider and more diverse range of texts would be included in this view than in a cultural heritage perspective. The key difference in belief within this model was that it emphasized pluralism, diversity, and challenge to established cultural authority. The cultural analysis view had largely originated in university departments in the 1970s and 1980s and was influenced by radical philosophies and by feminist theories.

The intention of the Cox Report was to be inclusive and to recognize the diverse beliefs about English; therefore, the five views were presented as alternatives, all of equal validity in contributing to good practice in the subject. The report did not offer much discussion of how the five views had originated, nor of their relationship to each other. This is understandable when one of its aims was to emphasize consensus in relation to English – where different opinions could be identified but, nonetheless, could be accommodated within the same framework.

As indicated earlier in this chapter, the Cox Report largely succeeded in establishing consensus among English teachers over the proposed National Curriculum order for English. Although there were problems in the five views being presented as alternatives (Poulson, 1991), its inclusiveness reassured teachers that the new National Curriculum would not be narrow and overly prescriptive. There was an overwhelming feeling that the content and structure of English proposed for the National Curriculum were acceptable. A research study investigating the first year of implementation of assessment of English in the National Curriculum at Key Stage 3, in secondary schools (e.g. Radnor *et al.*, 1995, p. 329), showed that by 1992 many secondary teachers had embraced the English curriculum detailed in the Cox Report, and that it had gained strong support, as indicated in the interviews with heads of departments and teachers in a range of comprehensive schools in different parts of England. The comments below, from heads of English in three schools, are illustrative of the positive regard in which the Cox recommendations were held:

> Most people I know felt the Cox Report vindicated the best of good practice that we had all learned ... It was wonderful when this guy who had actually been one of the authors of the Black Papers suddenly said, 'Well, actually this is good practice.' We felt great. (Head of English, Riverside)

I think we are still at the stage where we are saying we liked [the] Cox [Report] and we're prepared to produce schemes of work to fit in with the programmes of study. (Head of department, St Boniface, 1992)

People felt affirmed by the Cox Report – the five views. (Head of department, Christopher Marlowe, 1992)

The Cox Committee had achieved a number of things that were potentially problematic: it had presented programmes of study for English that included progression for pupils from 5 to 16; it had identified levels of attainment for pupils at the ages of 7, 11, 14 and 16; and it had structured the content of English in a way that was acceptable to most people, and avoided a separation between language and literature. However, as our research study began in the autumn of 1992, and the first interviews were done, disquiet was already being voiced among teachers about government proposals to revise the original National Curriculum for English presented in the Cox Report. There was particular concern about the proposals for assessment at Key Stage 3. During 1992–93, this feeling of disquiet grew, and turned into an unambiguous resistance to the revised English order in the National Curriculum. By June 1993 the consensus established by the Cox Report had been undermined and English teachers were boycotting Key Stage 3 tests. What, then, had caused this change in so short a period of time? The answer to this question lies in the determination of the government of the time to ensure that English in the National Curriculum had a more traditional and authoritarian emphasis, which more clearly reflected its own values. The issues of language, and in particular grammar and spoken standard English, were forefronted in proposals to revise the English order, even though these were some of the more contentious aspects of the English curriculum.

# 4

# Political interventions in English

The Cox Committee had done what few thought possible at the time: it had reconciled government demands for tighter control of the English curriculum in schools with proposals that were acceptable to most teachers. It had also appeared to reconcile a range of differing beliefs about the nature and purpose of English in primary and secondary schools. In spite of teachers' support for the Cox Committee recommendations, the early 1990s were marked by dissent and controversy about English in the school curriculum, particularly in secondary schools, which ultimately led to the boycott of the National Curriculum Key Stage tests in 1993. The move to boycott the tests was led initially by English teachers and the London Association for the Teaching of English (LATE), then supported by others throughout the country. As opposition gathered force it was also supported by the teaching unions, headteachers and parents. The reason for the rapid change of climate from one of consensus to open dispute was a deliberate attempt to rewrite the English curriculum to reflect the views of a small number of right-wing individuals in the government and among ministerial advisers. This chapter will consider the specific political agenda of the time, and how it was realized through manipulation of the curriculum and examination agencies. Four issues were central to the dispute: the teaching of standard English; grammar; the place of Shakespeare in the English curriculum; and assessment arrangements.

## Government resistance to the Cox English curriculum

If the consensus about English within the new National

Curriculum established by the Cox Report was accepted by the professional association, NATE, and by teachers, it was accepted much more reluctantly by the government that had established the working group and had set curriculum reform in motion as part of the 1988 Education Reform Act. On publication, the report received much media publicity, some of it similar to that which had greeted the publication of the Bullock Report in 1975. The Cox Report did not offer a simple populist solution to the teaching of English within the new National Curriculum, and therefore it was treated scathingly by the right-wing press. The focus for attack was, in this instance, not so much literacy and reading standards, but more the issue of standard English and grammar. Cox's personal account of involvement in both the Kingman Committee and the National Curriculum working group offers an insight into the politicization of English teaching in recent years and into the political processes at work. It must be remembered that this is Cox's personal account of events: none the less, it offers an interesting inside perspective from a key actor in the events of the time and a supplement to the evidence of official documents, letters, speeches and press reports. The political manoeuvring over the English curriculum is highlighted in Cox's account of the selection of the members of the National Curriculum working group by the then Secretary of State for Education on the basis of his belief (in many cases erroneous) that each supported Conservative political aims, or had traditional or right-wing views on education. Professor Cox acknowledged that his role as editor of the Black Paper series in the late 1960s and 1970s had influenced his appointment (Cox, 1991, p. 4). He also maintained that when membership of the working group was announced, Kenneth Baker and Angela Rumbold were accused of choosing political appointees to reflect the Prime Minister's Conservative ideology. In reality, the way in which the choices were made was rather more haphazard and humorous:

> Roald Dahl, the children's writer, attended the first meeting, admitted he hated committees, and never reappeared. Apparently Mr Baker had met him on a social occasion, and had been impressed by his traditionalist views.... Roger Samways, Adviser for English and

47

Drama in Dorset, was very progressive in his outlook, holding views about children's learning which were anathema to most right-wing Conservatives. Roger recounted ... what happened when he was interviewed by Mr Baker. They spent the first ten minutes talking about Thomas Hardy, because Roger came from Dorset, and then Mr Baker read passages from the Kingman Report which was still unpublished, and asked if Roger agreed. Unsure about what Kingman really advocated, Roger could only mutter polite words of assent (*ibid.*, pp. 4–5)

Cox maintained that in spite of their strongly held ideological beliefs, the politicians were amateur in their approach to ensuring a politically acceptable curriculum for English:

[they were] instinctively confident that common sense was sufficient to guide them in making judgements about the professional standing of the interviewees [for the working group]. I suspect that they did not realise that words like 'grammar' or 'progressive' reflect very different meanings according to context, or that the language of educational discourse had changed radically since they were at school. (*ibid.*, p. 6)

Grammar and standard English became the focus of press comment as soon as the report was published; Cox reported that Kenneth Baker felt that insufficient attention had been given to the teaching of grammar. In the proposals, printed at the front of the report, the Secretary of State asked that 'the programmes of study be strengthened to give greater emphasis to the place of grammatical structure and terminology (letter printed at the front of the Report of the working group for English (DES, 1988)). Articles in the press suggested that the report had ignored grammar. The *Daily Mail* (16.11.1988) published an article that began, 'Bad grammar is acceptable for schoolchildren, an official report recommended yesterday.' The *Evening Standard* similarly had a headline which read, 'Baker's Hard Man "Soft" on Grammar', and the *Mail on Sunday* had a headline which announced, 'Thatcher Furious with "Trendy" Experts', and began the article by stating that 'A report telling schools to ignore English teaching in favour of trendy methods has infuriated Mrs Thatcher' (13.11.88). The majority press reaction to the recommendations in the Cox Report echoes many of the assertions that were made in the period when the Bullock Report was published in 1975, as discussed in the previous chapter, and which preceded and followed the Callaghan Ruskin College speech in 1976. More than twenty years had elapsed and, most ironic, the chairperson of the working group was the chief editor of the Black Papers, which during the earlier period had presented an influential critique of the comprehensive reorganization of secondary schools and progressive teaching methods. Whatever changes of opinion Brian Cox might have had between 1977 and 1988, he was still an unlikely subject for the epithet 'trendy'.

There followed several attempts to ensure that a stronger emphasis was placed upon aspects of the subject and ways of teaching which even in 1921 had been called into question by the Newbolt Report, and had been rejected as inappropriate by each subsequent major report dealing with the teaching of English. From the early 1990s, Conservative politicians, and their advisers, pursued a narrow and dogmatic definition of standard English, grammar and literary heritage. One of the most important ways in which they did this was by determining or influencing the membership of key agencies responsible for the implementation of the National Curriculum and assessment. One of the first examples of the shift from consensus to confrontation was the suppression in 1991 by the Department of Education and Science of the training and development materials produced by the Language in the National Curriculum project (LINC), arising from the recommendation of the Kingman Report that teachers in both primary and secondary schools would need in-service training in teaching knowledge about language.

The LINC project had a clear theoretical grounding in modern linguistics and by no means promoted the sort of approach to grammar teaching that might have found favour with government ministers. Underpinning its work were theories which acknowledged that language was a social phenomenon and was also dynamic – changing over time and according to the context of its use. Such an approach made connections between language, social power, gender relations and culture. No official explanation was ever given as to why the LINC project materials were never published or disseminated. Unofficially, when the materials were presented for publication, the Department of Education and Science indicated to the LINC steering committee that there was too strong an emphasis on the social and cultural aspects of language and linguistic diversity and not enough emphasis on standard English. It was also suggested that the materials were unsuitable for use with pupils in school – a use for which they had never been intended. The suppression of these materials, intended for in-service work with teachers, marked a political change in approach. Cox's (1991) description of the *ad hoc* appointment to committees of those considered sympathetic to right-wing ideology seemed to have been replaced by more direct intervention in the rewriting of the statutory order for English and in the arrangements for National Curriculum assessment.

## The role of political pressure groups in rewriting National Curriculum English

From 1991, a number of important changes took place in the composition of the curriculum and assessment agencies, the National Curriculum Council (NCC) and the School Examination and Assessment Council (SEAC), which enabled this to be achieved more easily. A number of officers considered to be politically neutral were replaced by people who had a clear political allegiance, many of whom had served as policy advisers to successive Conservative governments or were members of right-wing think-tanks and pressure groups. Duncan Graham was replaced as the chairperson and chief executive at the NCC; he was succeeded by David Pascall, a former member of Margaret Thatcher's Downing Street Policy Unit. Pascall chose members for NCC who were closely associated with right-wing Conservative pressure groups, such as Graham Mackenzie, Brian Hutchinson and David Regan, who was also a member of the Educational Research Trust, directed by John Marks and advised by Brian Griffiths. At SEAC, Philip Halsey was replaced by Brian Griffiths (Baron Griffiths of Fforestfach), formerly Head of Thatcher's Downing Street Policy Unit and also a member of the Centre for Policy Studies. Within SEAC, other appointees had an equally right-wing bias: John Marks chaired the Mathematics committee and John Marenbon, another member of the Centre for Policy Studies, chaired the English committee.

The influence of right-wing pressure groups and think-tanks on the reshaping of the English curriculum was strong. In an address to one of these groups, John Marks argued that the teaching of English had become the main ideological battleground in Britain for those who wanted to politicize education in a left-wing direction. (Cox, 1995, p. 33). However, the evidence suggested that the politicization of education was in much less danger from those with ideological leanings to the left than from those with strong leanings towards the far right. The Centre for Policy Studies, in particular, had concentrated its attention on aspects of the English curriculum. Parallels may be seen between the content of pamphlets written for the Centre for Policy Studies by Oliver Letwin, John Marenbon and Sheila Lawlor and some of the changes to the English curriculum that were being pushed through by those of similar political persuasion on committees within the curriculum and assessment agencies. An examination of claims made in Centre for Policy Studies publications reveals some of the means by which a particular set of views were produced and represented as though they were universal common sense.

In *English, Our English*, Marenbon argued that, within English teaching, there was an orthodoxy which regarded it as a conceptual error to speak of correct English, and which rejected the idea of a literary heritage (Marenbon, 1987, p. 5). According to Marenbon's criteria, this new orthodoxy in English teaching, which he attacked, would have included most of those involved in the teaching and inspection of the subject and many academic linguists. In fact, it seemed to include anyone who did not share his priorities in the teaching of English, or his political philosophy. He also dismissed descriptive approaches to the study of language, arguing that what was needed was *prescription*: rules relating to the correct use of syntax and lexis. Marenbon also argued that those who saw grammar as a description of language and its use had misunderstood the nature of grammar (*ibid.*, p. 20). The assertion is as arrogant as it is bizarre, particularly when the very issue of descriptive and prescriptive approaches to grammar was discussed as long ago as 1921 in the Newbolt Report. The members of that

Committee, who included Henry Newbolt, George Sampson, Caroline Spurgeon, F. S. Boas and Arthur Quiller-Couch, make unlikely candidates for inclusion in Marenbon's new orthodoxy in English teaching; none the less, the ideas about grammar so confidently asserted in *English, Our English* had been treated with caution in 1921. In the Newbolt Report, the issue of grammar teaching was identified as problematic and complex, with differences of opinion being offered by the witnesses.

Lawlor (1990) and Letwin (1988) also addressed the issue of English teaching and literacy, constructing arguments that were almost identical to those of Marenbon. Indeed, the proposals for an English curriculum in *The Correct Core* (Lawlor, 1990) were remarkably similar to the proposed revisions to the English National Curriculum order. Marenbon, Lawlor and Letwin claimed to draw upon established traditional authority, and many of the publications of right-wing pressure groups such as the Centre for Policy Studies are in a style reminiscent of nineteenth-century texts. However, close examination of the sources of that very tradition does not support the claims of individuals such as Marenbon and Lawlor to be the natural successors to nineteenth-century public figures such as Matthew Arnold or James Kay-Shuttleworth – who, for their own time, had more forward-thinking views on education. An example may be found in the section of the Newbolt Report dealing with the differences between descriptive and prescriptive approaches to grammar, which clearly contradicts assertions made by members of the Centre for Policy Studies and also by Secretaries and Ministers of State for Education. The Newbolt Report acknowledged the complexity of the issue of grammar and language teaching within the English curriculum and recognized that there were a number of different perspectives on it. Letwin, Marenbon, Lawlor and others selectively reconstructed their own version of nineteenth- and early twentieth-century ideas and beliefs about education and society. A detailed examination of the arguments serves to highlight a refusal to consider informed evidence, the intellectual barrenness of the ideas, and the misconceptions that were so influential in reshaping the curriculum and assessment arrangements in English.

The obvious politicization of the school curriculum and its

assessment, with English as a particular focus, did not go unchallenged. Brian Cox (1995) suggested that the political manipulation of the curriculum and assessment agencies worked against democratic procedures in ensuring that a small number of like-minded people with extreme political views were in control:

> July 1991 proved a bad month for British democracy. I played a small but symbolic part in events which enabled a small, right-wing pressure group to take over the National Curriculum, though at the time I did not appreciate the significance of what was happening....
>
> What is so disturbing about these events is the ease with which such a small group of like-minded campaigners were able to take over the National Curriculum, with little public knowledge of what was happening.... All these right-wingers were sincere, honest and passionately committed to their educational beliefs. They were willing to work hard; the results of their labours were to cause major disruption in our schools for several years (Cox, 1995, pp. 22, 28)

Cox outlined the process by which a case was constructed for the revision of the original National Curriculum statutory order for English, in spite of substantial evidence from a number of independent sources that the original Cox curriculum was supported by teachers and was generally working well in schools. His observations were supported by a later research study on the implementation of the National Curriculum for English undertaken at the University of Exeter in 1992–93, referred to in Chapter 3 (Radnor *et al.*, 1995; Poulson *et al.*, 1996). However, reasoned argument did not win the day. Kenneth Clarke, the Secretary of State for Education, and his successor, John Patten, were content to listen to Marenbon, Lawlor, Letwin and other right-wing views and to ignore those who suggested that a revision of the English curriculum would not be helpful.

In July 1992, the National Curriculum Council submitted to the Secretary of State for Education a case for the revision of the English order. In a letter that prefaced the document, the then chairperson of NCC, David Pascall, warned that English was a controversial subject which 'attracts strong and polarized opinions' (NCC, 1992, p. 1). He acknowledged the popularity and general acceptance of the existing order for English: 'We have given careful consideration to the argument that any decision to revise what is a popular Order will undermine morale and prejudice the progress which has been made since the introduction of National Curriculum English' (*ibid.*, p. 2). None the less, *National Curriculum English: The Case for Revising the Order* stated that there was a need for a stronger focus on standard English. It suggested, 'There is a case, therefore, for strengthening the references to mastery of standard English in the statements of attainment and programmes of study, and more specifically, for requiring children to use standard English before Level 5' (*ibid.*, p. 11). It argued for a clearer element of grammatical knowledge, rather than knowledge about how language is used:

> pupils still need to develop a better understanding of grammatical terms. Part of the problem is that the Order, as it is currently drafted, takes a broad view of what children should know about the way in which language works. Teachers can give equal weight, for example, to studies of accent and dialect, on the one hand, and to the teaching of grammatical terms and syntax, on the other. (*ibid.*, p. 28)

It also indicated a need to specify the kind of literature to which pupils should be introduced: 'The issue is whether the Order needs to provide a more explicit definition of the literature pupils should read in order to further the objective of encouraging wide reading and an appreciation of good literature' (*ibid.*, p. 22). In September 1992, Patten accepted the advice of the National Curriculum Council to revise the English order, and he set up a review group to do this. There was considerable concern among English teachers about the possible outcome of a revised National Curriculum for English.

## A boycott of Key Stage 3 tests: the impact of proposals for National Curriculum assessment of English

A narrower and more dogmatic stance towards the teaching of literature came not so much through revision of the statutory curriculum as through the proposed assessment arrangements for English, particularly at Key Stage 3. In the Exeter Key Stage 3 study, heads of English departments in eight comprehensive schools in diverse areas throughout England were interviewed in the autumn of 1992, and whole English departments in spring 1993. Almost all the teachers expressed grave reservations about political intervention in the school curriculum. Many questioned the degree to which those responsible for rewriting the English order and producing the assessment tasks understood English teaching in the average comprehensive school. Teachers in this study felt strongly about introducing Shakespeare to pupils at Key Stage 3, and the ways in which the new assessment arrangements would actually serve to restrict the amount and quality of that work. It was clear that many schools already taught Shakespeare and other pre-twentieth-century literary texts with enthusiasm to pupils of all abilities and backgrounds at Key Stages 3 and 4. Many described exciting and innovative ways of teaching classic literary texts, which made them accessible to modern teenagers, as indicated in the comments of the two teachers below:

> There's a member of the department who's been teaching for years, who's taken on *The Tempest* blithely with a mixed-ability class doing such lovely innovative stuff ... and brought it truly alive. (Head of English, Christopher Marlowe, autumn 1992)

> I think good schools in London and elsewhere have been teaching difficult texts to year 8, 9 and 10 now for a long time. It's what you do with the text that's important. (Teacher, Tree Vale, March 1993)

Heads of English departments and other teachers expressed their concern about the confusion caused by the School Examination and Assessment Council (SEAC), which had sent out lists of prescribed texts after most well-organized departments had ordered set texts for the year and had planned schemes of work. In particular, there was concern throughout the winter of 1992 and spring of 1993 about the narrow range of texts and tasks that were likely to be set for pupils at Key Stage 3, particularly in relation to Shakespeare. It was felt that the narrowness of choice, and the lateness with which schools had been informed of the prescribed texts, worked against the best interests of both pupils and teachers. One head of department interviewed indicated the negative impact of the assessment arrangements on the teaching of Shakespeare in her school:

> When we teach Shakespeare, we teach it to all of them ... last year I
> evolved a very good unit of work on *The Tempest* which I used with
> Year 9 pupils. It got them into the text ... they got into paraphrasing
> ... there was a lot of textual work involved, where pupils who had
> never dreamed they could handle Shakespeare could work with the
> language. It was wonderful, and I planned to do it this year; I can't, it's
> not one of the prescribed texts. But we don't have time now to evolve
> a similar unit for one of those prescribed texts. (Head of department,
> Riverside, September 1992)

The SEAC requirements that pupils be entered in tiers, according
to ability, for the Key Stage 3 assessments appeared to indicate
that fewer pupils would be given access to Shakespeare and other
pre-twentieth-century texts in their entirety, rather than as
selected extracts. Teachers were also concerned that imaginative
and analytic approaches to teaching Shakespeare to pupils of all
abilities would be replaced by approaches that prepared children
to answer exam questions rather than to extend their knowledge
and understanding of literature:

> I have a Year 9 class who got a tremendous amount from Shakespeare
> but [in the Key Stage 3 SAT] they are not being given a variety of
> questions around it ... they are not being challenged ... they will be
> asked to write about one particular extract or give one short answer
> or fill in words in a box ... that is the most reductive way of teaching
> and learning Shakespeare. (Teacher, Tree Vale, spring 1993)

Schools were extremely concerned that English teaching was
being led by assessment requirements, contrary to statements
about the relationship between the curriculum and assessment
arrangements set out in the early documents issued by the
National Curriculum Task Group on Assessment and Testing
(TGAT). Moreover, the sample questions for the Key Stage 3
tests, which SEAC sent to schools in late 1992, were so dull and
narrow in their scope they alienated some teachers who might
otherwise have worked to accommodate National Curriculum
assessment:

> When the papers were leaked [the sample Key Stage 3 SAT
> questions] and we saw exactly what kind of questions, the anger was
> uniform, and for me, it has changed my line totally about SATs,

because up to that point I had been prepared to do [them]. (Teacher, Riverside, March 1993)

Similarly, a literature anthology, on which pupils were to be assessed in the Key Stage 3 SATs, published early in 1993, aroused contempt and fury on the part of all those concerned with the teaching of English from primary schools to universities. It was regarded as limited and mediocre in content, and included poems and other extracts from literature which might have been found in anthologies used in Edwardian elementary schools. For example, the anthology contained an extract from Johnson's *Rasselas*, John Masefield's *Sea Fever* and Wordsworth's *Daffodils*. Of its backward-looking nostalgia, Graham Frater, previously HMI staff inspector for English, wrote:

> The mood is so relentlessly retrospective that even the youngest living writer (d.o.b. 1944) is represented by a poem entitled 'Yesterday'... A conspiracy theorist could be forgiven for imagining that SEAC was seeking to make literature unappealing for fourteen year olds.... This anthology, with its ill-sorted materials and the problems it poses for fair and effective assessment is part of the price which pupils and schools must pay for an unedifying concoction of blind dogma and contingent, quick-fit decision-making. (*Education*, 22.1.93, p. 5).

The eventual publication of the revised English order in 1993 did nothing to alleviate the increasing disquiet at all levels of English teaching, and served as a focus for opposition. Statements of Attainment that dealt with spoken standard English, which was defined as grammatically correct English, posed particular problems for assessment. Teachers in the Exeter study questioned how they would assess whether pupils used spoken standard English, as exemplified in the comments below:

> I'm certainly worried about this business of standard English, because it seems to me that creeping in with it is the idea of RP [received pronunciation] as well. (Teacher, Riverside, March 1993)

> It seems to me that the rewritten order for English, with its insistence on children speaking standard English and only standard English, is one of the major concerns that I have as an English teacher. I see

absolutely nothing wrong with teaching children how to write and up
to a point how to speak standard English – although if that becomes
the only form of ... writing and speaking, then it is quite wrong. ...
Speaking and listening are ephemeral things to assess anyway ... but
to actually assess use of standard English ... is prescriptive, it is
culturally divisive and ... it would certainly devalue and marginalise
any child from a working-class or ethnically diverse background who
couldn't easily speak standard English. There are all sorts of
assumptions about standard English: it is somehow white, educated,
middle-class and culturally secure. (Teacher of English, Tree Vale,
March 1993)

There was also concern among the teachers who participated in
this research that instead of a broad concept of language study and
knowledge about language, such as that contained in the first
version of the National Curriculum, based on the model
recommended by the Kingman Committee, the revised order for
English defined language study largely in terms of grammatical
structure:

I think what they [government ministers] have in mind when they talk
about knowledge about language is clause analysis and parts of
speech. (Teacher, Queen Caroline's, March 1993)

I just think the government sees KAL [knowledge about language] as
being a study of grammar, and I think in the new orders that's how it
is. (Teacher, Moordale, March 1993)

During the autumn and winter of 1992 and the spring of 1993,
opposition to the rewritten English curriculum and the plans for
Key Stage 3 tests grew, not only among secondary school English
teachers, but also among headteachers, school governors and
parents. There were a number of organized campaigns against the
proposed Key Stage 3 tests in June 1993. One of the most
successful was that organized by the London Association of
Teachers of English (LATE), which wrote to all heads of English in
secondary schools in England and Wales in November 1992 and
gained the support of approximately 700 heads of English
departments, in both maintained and independent schools in
England. A collection of letters of support from these teachers,
*Voices from the Classroom* (Wilks, 1993), was published. In it John

Wilks, the chair of LATE, stated that English teachers from every part of the country had written back, sharing the same concerns and expressing anger at the government actions. He described how replies were received from state and independent schools, from inner-city, suburban and rural schools, from comprehensive and selective schools; and he pointed out that not one letter had supported the government's decision (*ibid.*, 1993, p. 3).

The comments published in the LATE booklet echoed those of the heads of department and teachers of English who were interviewed in 1992, and again in the spring and summer of 1993. The determination of the Secretary of State to push through curriculum and assessment proposals for English without heed to other opinion, either from within the teaching profession or from elsewhere, was a major factor leading to the widespread support for a boycott of the tests in June 1993. Teachers in the schools in the Exeter study indicated their concern at the narrowness and dogmatism of the political agenda for English, believing that it was based not on an informed perspective, but on a nostalgic hankering after a lost golden age of a static hierarchical society. The political agenda for English centred on the issues of standard English, defined as grammatically correct English; on the replacement of knowledge about language with a teaching of grammatical structure; and on a narrow and old-fashioned selection of literary texts. Teachers felt that underlying the political interference with the English curriculum was an assumption that they could not be trusted and were not doing their job properly. Their feelings about this were strong:

> I don't think it is about teaching English, or about language. I think it is political reaction; I really feel strongly that is what it's about; and it's also about disempowering people who don't belong. (English teacher, Tree Vale, March 1993)

> I think there's a sense about a lot of this that we don't feel that the people who are telling us what to do understand what they are actually asking ...

> Or that they understand the nature of teaching children. ... If I felt that they really knew what they were talking about, I might welcome it a bit more. (Two English teachers, Moordale, March 1993)

## An attempt at conciliation: the Dearing review of the curriculum

The outcome of the boycott of tests, either direct or indirect, was a change of direction. The Secretary of State for Education, John Patten, was replaced by the rather more conciliatory Gillian Shephard, while David Pascall, the chairperson of SEAC, was replaced by Sir Ron Dearing, with the NCC and SEAC being merged to form one agency, the School Curriculum and Assessment Authority (SCAA) in April 1993. Although Shephard had immediately promised to act upon the proposals of the proposed Dearing review of the National Curriculum which was to report in December 1993, the composition of the newly formed curriculum and assessment agency remained largely unchanged, except that John Marenbon had resigned from the English committee in May 1993. The new working group constituted to revise the English statutory order included such people as Arthur Pollard and Anthony O'Hear, who were also closely associated with right-wing pressure groups and had advised Conservative ministers. The continuing dismissal of professional and expert advice on curriculum policy in English was highlighted in a leading article in the *Times Educational Supplement* by members of the advisory groups constituted as part of the Dearing review of the National Curriculum in 1993. It pointed out that all eleven members of the group appointed to advise on what children should learn up to the age of 7 had written to its chairperson, Sir Ron Dearing, complaining that their advice on English had been ignored. Against their advice, there was an even greater emphasis on standard English. These criticisms followed similar ones by some members of the English advisory committee, who had claimed that much of their advice had been either ignored or changed beyond recognition (*TES*, 20.5.93).

Members of curriculum advisory groups who were less closely affiliated to the politics of the government were critical of the insistence upon standard English, and also of the way in which the evidence from consultation on the curriculum was ignored. This appeared to be the case even after the promised review of the National Curriculum, presided over by Sir Ron Dearing. Alastair

West, a member of the new working group for English, argued that the review of the curriculum was at risk of becoming an exercise in nostalgia. He expressed regret that so many of the English group's recommendations had been rejected, and suggested that Brian Cox's fears about the politicization of English remained well founded, even though the executive of the School Curriculum and Assessment Authority (SCAA) insisted that there had been no ministerial intervention in the revisions to the proposals made by the advisory group, and that the Secretary of State had respected the autonomy and independence of the SCAA (*TES*, 20.5.93).

The resulting revised curriculum order for English was much reduced in size and detail. The three strands of reading, writing, and speaking and listening were retained as the main organizational structure of the curriculum, with an additional strand dealing with language study which emphasized standard English and aspects of grammar, punctuation and spelling. Although a compromise, this additional strand did not always relate coherently to the other three strands, and areas of overlap were evident. However, the brevity of the statements of attainment and programmes of study meant that it was actually less prescriptive than the first revised English order in 1993. Another important difference was the revision of the assessment tasks at Key Stage 3, which took account of some of the issues to which teachers had been so strongly opposed in 1993.

As discussed in detail in this chapter, underlying the dispute about English in 1992–93 were important differences in belief and philosophy between the majority of English teachers in schools in England and a small but politically influential group of people who informed and shaped government policy on education. The differences were not about the relative importance of language or literature in the school English curriculum, nor about the purpose of English in the school curriculum, but rather about the nature of knowledge and the most appropriate ways of teaching and assessing English. The ideas of a few right-wing individuals were promoted, including the belief that there is a fixed body of worthwhile knowledge to be learned which remains relatively unchanged from one generation to another and that worthwhile literature is that which has stood the test of time, or simply has

61

been around for a long time. Although the members of the Centre for Policy Studies attempted to engage with questions of literary value, they did so in an inconsistent and often contradictory way. Ironically, many English teachers would agree with the importance of teaching Shakespeare and other pre-twentieth-century texts to pupils, although they would disagree on the most appropriate and effective way of doing this. It was certainly the case that the English departments in the schools participating in the Exeter study prioritized the teaching of literature rather than the direct teaching of language. However, that is itself a complex issue, and will be examined in Chapter 5. An attachment to the study of grammatical forms, and to promoting the teaching of standard spoken English, results from a belief that language is unchanging, and that the job of teachers is to prescribe and maintain correct forms. The underlying theme of the political manipulation of English by pressure groups was to establish the teaching of English as a narrow and fixed body of literary texts; to promote spoken standard English, defined as correct English; and to ensure the teaching of prescriptive grammatical rules. The intention was that these things would be assessed by traditional examinations in which there were right and wrong answers. In such developments can be glimpsed the desire for a fixed and secure world in which everyone knows his or her place; in which there is clearly established authority and prescribed rules; and in which language and its use reflect a prescribed, authoritarian social order.

The reform of the National Curriculum order for English was politically motivated. However, the argument was not just about political differences; it was also about different value systems, and ways of seeing the world. Government ministers and their advisers seemed to want to return to a society of fifty or more years ago. They also believed that learning involved the assimilation of fixed bodies of knowledge and facts, which were handed down largely unchanged from one generation to another. There were many teachers, parents and school governors who were rather less enthusiastic about returning to the world of fifty years ago, and who regarded what pupils learned as more than the unquestioning assimilation of bodies of knowledge. Nowhere was the conflict between two very different value-systems more keenly felt than in relation to the teaching of English in English and Welsh schools in the early 1990s.

Since then, there have been other forms of political intervention in the teaching of English, most notably in relation to literacy in primary schools. The Labour government's national literacy strategy, with its proposals for a uniform way of teaching reading and writing within a highly specified daily literacy hour, has also proved to be controversial. Not only is the content of the curriculum prescribed in detail, but so are the teaching methods to be used. A further point is that in January 1998, David Blunkett, Secretary of State for Education, announced that for Key Stages 1 and 2, the National Curriculum orders for non-core subjects would be relaxed in order to allow primary schools to concentrate on literacy and numeracy, and to achieve the specified targets. The proposal acknowledged the increased demands made upon primary schools by implementation of the literacy and numeracy strategies. It was also controversial in that the primary curriculum was effectively slimmed down to core subjects, with particular emphasis on literacy and numeracy. This was a move that many people felt to be a return to the sort of narrow curriculum found in Victorian and Edwardian elementary schools in Britain. The issue is genuinely problematic; there are strong arguments in favour of primary schools prioritizing the teaching of literacy and numeracy. One of the strongest of these is that, unless pupils have adequate competence in reading, writing and number they will not have access to many areas of knowledge. There are equally strong arguments in favour of primary school pupils having access to a curriculum which consists of more than just the basics – a curriculum which includes the arts, humanities and practical subjects.

# 5

# Language in the English curriculum

One of the most controversial aspects of English has been the teaching of language. The continuing debate about this part of the subject is often puzzling to those not involved in teaching. A clearer understanding of the controversies may be gained by identifying the different underlying assumptions in the arguments about language. The previous chapter identified two areas that have been particularly controversial in relation to the National Curriculum: the place of grammar, and the promotion of standard spoken English. It is common for discussion of language to be reduced to generalized statements about grammar, standard English, spelling and punctuation. For example, a frequent assertion is that formal grammar lessons and emphasis on correctness in pupils' use of language would lead to higher standards of literacy. In fact there is no evidence to suggest that this would be the case; and there is substantial evidence to suggest that such an approach would have little or no impact on standards of literacy.

## The place of grammar

Chapter 2 indicated the ways in which English developed as a subject in the school curriculum from the end of the nineteenth century. Victorian and Edwardian elementary schools provided a cheap and basic education that concentrated on numeracy and literacy. The elementary school curriculum included a strong element of rote learning of grammatical rules and parsing of sentences. The aim was inculcation of a set of rules for the correct use of language, rather than enabling pupils to understand how language worked. Learning grammatical rules was reinforced through mechanical exercises intended to ensure that pupils could form sentences accurately. As outlined in Chapter 2, a more liberal notion of English teaching in elementary schools gradually began to emerge through the efforts of individuals such as Matthew Arnold and members of the English Association.

The Newbolt Committee had recognized that there were different ways of thinking about English language and its teaching, and that these had conflicting implications for practice. In Chapter 4, I argued that underlying the notions about language, grammar and standard English held by individuals such as John Marenbon and John Honey was a belief that the primary purpose of language teaching in schools ought to be the prescription of rules for correct use of English. Interestingly, discussion of grammar within the Newbolt Report was strikingly modern: it centred on the differences between descriptive and prescriptive approaches to language study, and considered the place of grammar teaching within the English curricula of different types of educational institutions. It enquired very sensibly as to the purpose of studying grammar; for which sorts of pupils it was suited, and for which it was not. It came to the conclusion that there was no clear consensus among the witnesses consulted, as indicated in the extract from the report given below:

> Dr Ballard told us that grammar does not provide a general mental training, or enable teachers to eradicate solecisms, or afford any help in composition work, and he argued therefrom that grammar teaching is futile ... in the elementary school. On the other hand, Mr Barton's complaint was that by neglecting grammar the elementary school is throwing aside an instrument which 'is vital to all linguistic study'. The witnesses were using the word 'grammar' in two different senses; Dr Ballard was attacking the old conception of grammar, as a body of rules which were supposed to be binding upon all who would speak or write 'correctly' – in short, grammar as legislation; Mr Barton was asking ... to lay the foundations of grammar, in the true sense, that is a body of facts about language in general and English in particular – in short grammar as science. This divergence in meaning takes us at once to the heart of the problem. For why do we teach and learn grammar? The answer may be given in the words of one of our

greatest living authorities on language, Professor Wyld, who writes ...
'It is quite a mistaken idea to suppose that English Grammars are
written to teach English people how to speak their own language. ...
A grammar book does *not* attempt to teach people how they *ought* to
speak, but, on the contrary, unless it is a very bad or very old work, it
merely states how, as a matter of fact, certain people *do* speak at the
time at which it is written.' (Board of Education, 1921, pp. 280–1)

The issue of who should learn grammar in school was dealt with
pragmatically. The Newbolt Report highlighted a major misconcep-
tion about the relationship between learning grammatical rules
and the improvement of pupils' use of spoken and written English,
which has continued to inform debates about the teaching of
language up to the present time:

> If grammar is the necessary introduction to all linguistic study, then
> grammar must be taught to all who are making a study of language. ...
> If, on the other hand, a knowledge of grammar does little or nothing to
> improve the speaking and writing of the mother tongue, then it ceases
> to be essential for children who do not require any linguistic study.
> (*ibid.*, p. 282)

Another important point was made in connection with grammar
teaching. It argued that language, and grammar in particular, was
often taught badly, and there was much misunderstanding about
the structure of the language. It suggested that a reason for a lack
of interest in grammar in schools

> is to be found in the fact that grammar is usually taught for the wrong
> reasons, and reasons which a growing number of teachers are coming
> to see are wrong. In other words, grammar is still almost universally
> regarded a body of rules governing correct speech. (*ibid.*, pp. 282–3)

The arguments about forms of grammatical analysis, philology and
the teaching of language were complex, but the final recommendation of the committee was pragmatic: it was important for pupils to
learn grammar, but it should be studied in relation to its function,
rather than as a set of formal rules informing correct use of
English: 'We are of the opinion, therefore, that the case for
teaching a pure grammar, a grammar of function not form, is an
exceedingly strong one' (*ibid.*, p. 291).

Beliefs that grammar should be prescriptive continued to be powerful, despite the recommendations of the report. The linguists James and Lesley Milroy (1985) outlined a long-standing *complaint tradition* relating to grammar and standard English, in which the decline of English, or a worsening of the way in which it was used, had been claimed from the seventeenth and eighteenth centuries onwards, when English was codified and the early dictionaries compiled. The Milroys (*ibid.*, p. 55) argued that, in addition to a gradual standardization of the English language, there also developed an *ideology* of standard English which encouraged prescription in language use, based on the principle that there was one correct way of using words or grammatical structures. They also argued that within prescriptive views of language, standard English was regarded as inherently superior to other dialects – a notion that is misinformed. Reasons for promoting one unitary dialect above others often relate to a desire for uniformity, in order to make communication more efficient and to reduce the likelihood of miscomprehension. In addition, the move towards standardization and uniformity in language often relates to the formation of nation-states, national identity or colonial ambitions. This was the case with English in the nineteenth century.

The Milroys (*ibid.*) also argued that public discussion of the place of standard English in the school curriculum has been poorly informed and, in general, has not made a distinction between the language system and language in use. They also suggested that distinctions between standard written and spoken English have been inadequately emphasized. In the publications of right-wing pressure groups such as the Centre for Policy Studies and the National Council for Educational Standards (e.g. Marenbon, 1987; Honey, 1983), as detailed in the previous chapter, the distinctions have been either denied or ignored.

There is no doubt that prescriptive approaches to language, which emphasize grammatical rules and assert the correctness of standard English and its superiority to other dialects and usage, have led to much dull and uninspiring teaching. James Britton (1973, p. 13) described how he began his teaching career in a state grammar school in the early 1930s, when the controversy was not *whether*, but rather *how*, grammar would be taught. Many of the texts on grammar and language that were available then were modelled on primers for learning classical languages: they stated rules and gave paradigm cases to be learned and reinforced through exercises done by pupils. Britton commented that the best-selling textbooks were full of unproductive busy-work (*ibid.*, p. 13). He documented how he came to write his own grammar book, dissatisfied with the texts which were available then. Also in the 1930s, the British linguist John Firth identified flaws in the way in which language was studied (Firth, 1964). He blamed the educational provision of the 1870 Education Act and the elementary system for promoting the use of what he described as 'execrable grammars' for the young (*ibid.*, pp. 160, 195). Moreover, he argued that traditional school grammar books were based on deprecatory value judgements; and the emphasis placed on promoting artificial notions of good English in schools prevented them from turning out pupils who could put ideas into words simply and intelligibly. Firth identified the need for pupils to study language in a more purposeful way than was usually the case in the schools of the time. He argued that clearing the litter of generations of pedagogical mediocrity would provide more wholesome surroundings for children to learn about language. In order for this to happen, he indicated the need for modern linguistic study, including study of grammar, in university English degrees.

The absence of any clear alternative to prescriptive approaches to grammar teaching, and standard English based on notions of correctness, meant that once this approach was discredited as pointless and rejected by teachers, there was no systematic alternative approach to take its place (e.g. Milroy and Milroy, 1985). There have been numerous claims about a decline in the teaching of English language, and particularly grammar in schools since the 1960s, although the Bullock committee of inquiry found that the teaching of grammar was still common in British schools in the early 1970s. By no means suggesting that teachers should refrain from teaching the more formal aspects of language organization, the Bullock Report (DES, 1975) had questioned the effectiveness of grammar teaching in improving pupils' abilities in writing. It indicated, also, that in much of the evidence submitted to the committee of inquiry, the term 'grammar' often stood as a symbol for other aspects of language, and attitudes, that were not, strictly, grammatical issues at all:

> What, for that matter, is *meant* by grammar in the sense intended by those who suggest there should be more of it? In our discussions with teachers it became obvious that the term was often being used to include sentence construction, précis, paragraphing, vocabulary work, punctuation and much more besides. 'Grammar' has, of course, a highly specific and technical meaning, which we might roughly characterise as an analytical study of those formal arrangements of items in language by which utterances have meaning ...
>
> The traditional view of language teaching was, and indeed in many schools still is, prescriptive. It identified a correct set of forms and prescribed that these should be taught. As they were mastered the pupil would become a more competent writer and aspire to a standard of 'correctness' that would serve him for all occasions. Such a prescriptive view of language was based on a comparison with classical Latin, and it also mistakenly assumed an unchanging quality in both grammatical rules and word meaning in English. (*ibid.*, p. 169)

### What kind of language study?

The Bullock Report did not recommend a return to the formal and decontextualized teaching of grammar, or an emphasis on correct language use and standard English. Nor did it support the beliefs of people who wished for simple answers to the question of standards in literacy and language use. Instead, it emphasized every pupil's entitlement to access to standard forms of the language and the ability to use language appropriately in context:

> So we are not suggesting that the answer to improved standards is to be found in some such simple formula as: more grammar exercises, more formal speech training, more comprehension extracts. We believe that language competence grows incrementally, through an interaction of writing, talk, reading, and experience, the body of the resulting work forming an organic whole. (DES, 1975, p. 7)

However, in an earlier decade, Firth (1964) had indicated that a central problem related to the teaching of English language in schools in Britain was the knowledge base and academic allegiance of teachers. In the years since Firth made his observation, the content of degree courses in English has probably become even more strongly based on literary-textual study and criticism. The content of some courses, usually the more old-fashioned ones, included study of older forms of the English language such as Anglo-Saxon and the historical development of Indo-European languages. Few degree courses in English offer any systematic study of the structure and working of English; this is usually the province of the separate discipline of linguistics. Thus many specialist English teachers in secondary schools may have had little understanding of, or interest in, the structure of modern English beyond that gained in their school years. Similarly, primary school teachers are equally unlikely to have undertaken systematic language study. The Bullock Report attempted to address the lack of knowledge by recommending that all courses of training for teachers should include an element of language study, equivalent to 100 hours. However, the precise form and content of such study was left to the discretion of individual universities and colleges, among which there was considerable variation.

As indicated in Chapter 1, the HMI document *Curriculum Matters 1: English 5–16* (DES, 1984) found the teaching of language to be in need of more attention in primary and secondary schools, and suggested that this should be one of the aims of the English curriculum in schools. Referring to the area as knowledge about language, HMI suggested also that it was likely to be one of the most controversial aspects of the proposed curriculum. The later pamphlet, *English 5–16: The Responses to Curriculum Matters 1* (DES, 1986), summarized responses to the original proposals. It indicated that, as anticipated, the aspect of the English curriculum relating to 'knowledge about language' had prompted a good deal of disagreement and division (*ibid.*, p. 4), and that nothing had divided the respondents more than this issue (*ibid.*, p. 15). While pointing out that the original proposals in *English 5–16* had not supported prescriptive approaches to language learning, nor had it suggested a return to the teaching of grammatical analysis, *Responses to English 5–16* indicated how strong had been the opposition to such practices among respondents:

Colouring the whole debate were the experiences, recalled by many teachers, of exactly the old style of grammatical analysis headlined in some press reports. Those sit firmly in the memories of the majority as being 'tedious and useless' and research findings were invoked to reinforce the point. What was not widely noticed, however, was that the original paper also explicitly excluded this line of approach. (*ibid.*, p. 15)

Although a widespread and vigorous rejection of grammatical analysis, and of teaching the terminology listed in the objectives, was reported, *Responses to English 5–16* indicated that there was little agreement on what specific aspects of language should be taught to pupils and to prospective teachers. There was, however, general agreement among respondents that teachers should be expected to know about language and about language development in children (*ibid.*, p. 16). Some respondents had suggested that a substantial programme of in-service training and professional development would be needed for teachers to handle the language objectives listed in *English 5–16*, and that there had been a failure to implement the recommendations of the Bullock Report with regard to the training of prospective teachers.

One of the conclusions of *Responses to English 5-16* was that there was a gap between the *intent* to teach all children about the workings of language and agreement on the *means* by which this should, or could, be achieved. In order to address the gap between intention and practice, the document suggested that a

> concentrated and thorough public discussion of the issues is needed to focus opinion and guide policy formation about what should be taught about our language and what needs to be known by teachers and pupils. It is likely that the findings of such an enquiry would need to be followed up by a substantial investment in initial and in-service training and in the development of suitable teaching materials. (*ibid.*, p. 19)

However, the recommendation of a thorough and public discussion of the issues, in order to focus opinion and guide policy, seemed to ignore the powerful role of the media, particularly newspapers, in shaping the terms of any debate. This was all the more surprising because, in the first pages of *Responses to English 5–16*, HMI had pointed out, in some detail, the ways in which newspapers had misreported the original document in 1984 and had distorted its recommendations:

> the document was widely reported in the daily press in articles which were lively, variously informed, partial, superficial and mischievous in their representation of its contents. The press in general displayed an eagerness to use the document to criticise teachers and the standards achieved by pupils and there was much rosy sentiment about the past. The headlines in particular were unhelpful; they concentrated upon the issue of 'knowledge about language' which they reduced to 'grammar', and dubbed the recommendations as a call for a return to practices which were clearly and specifically criticised in the document itself. (*ibid.*, pp. 2–3)

It seems odd, given this level of awareness of the power of the media to shape any public discussion of language, and the unwillingness of much of the press to represent any liberal opinions, that HMI did not issue such a warning with the recommendation.

In the event, a committee of inquiry was established by the Secretary of State, Kenneth Baker, to be chaired by Sir John Kingman. Its terms of reference were to examine the teaching of English language and to recommend a model of the English language to inform teaching in schools. The Kingman Committee consisted of a distinguished, if diverse, group of people who had an interest or expertise in the English language and its teaching. It included three linguists (two of whom were professors), one professor of English literature, four writers, one member of the advisory service, two heads of English departments and one representative for teacher education. It is significant that there was no representation from the influential professional association, the National Association for the Teaching of English (NATE). The committee's report was, finally, unobjectionable, recommending a model of English consisting of four parts:

- forms of the language;
- communication and comprehension of English;
- the acquisition and development of language;
- historical and geographical variation in English.

As with the other two major reports dealing with English language this century, the Kingman Report did not offer a model of English that justified the position of those who believed the proper purpose of English was the prescriptive teaching of grammatical forms; and it also rejected the notion of a return to the teaching of decontextualized grammatical structures or sentence parsing:

> Nor do we see it as part of our task to plead for a return to old-fashioned grammar teaching and learning by rote. We have been impressed by the evidence we have received that this gave an inadequate account of the English language by treating it virtually as a branch of Latin, and constructing a rigid prescriptive code rather than a dynamic description of language in use. (DES, 1988, p. 3)

Throughout the report there was an attempt to balance a model of language in use with a more formal approach to the teaching and learning of language. Reactions to the Kingman Report varied, but overall the response within English teaching circles was lukewarm. The Kingman recommendations did not represent a reactionary view of language, or of the teaching of English, even if in places they may have sounded a little archaic and nostalgic. (As mentioned in Chapter 3, an editorial comment in autumn 1988 in *English in Education*, the journal of the National Association for the Teaching of English, regarded the Kingman Report as unlikely to be viewed as a benchmark in the teaching of English.) One of its recommendations was that all intending teachers of the primary age-range and intending teachers of secondary English should undertake a course of study that would enable them to acquire, understand and make use of knowledge about language according to the model proposed by the committee. In this respect, the Kingman Committee was both reiterating and extending recommendations made by the earlier Bullock Committee. Both sets of recommendations saw the education and professional development of teachers as crucial for any change in practice. In this respect both regarded change in practice as something to be achieved in the longer term, partly through changes in the attitudes and priorities of teachers.

The message about language study has been consistent throughout this century: that pupils need to have some knowledge of the workings of the English language; and that such knowledge should be related to the different ways and purposes for which English is used as a medium of communication. Thus the learning of formal elements of language, such as grammar, should be related to their function. A simple example is that verbs have different tenses, which are usually indicated in the particular formation of a word, such as the past-tense -ed ending; and the purpose of verbs having tenses is to mark shifts in reference to time in speech and writing. A further, important point is that teachers need to know how to teach the different aspects of language. Given this, it is regrettable that serious debate about the nature of language knowledge needed by teachers, and the best ways in which this should be presented to pupils, has been stifled and the issues distorted. The account of newspaper reporting of the content of the HMI *English 5–16: The Responses to Curriculum Matters 1* (DES, 1986) indicated how important questions had been trivialized and used as an opportunity to criticize teachers and make claims about the teaching of English language that were false and unhelpful. The role of the Centre for Policy Studies and other right-wing pressure groups in rewriting the National Curriculum so that the study of language was prescriptive and concerned largely with correct usage of grammatical structure was discussed in detail in Chapter 4.

### Teachers' conceptualization of language study

It needs to be emphasized that the problem of ensuring that teachers have the appropriate knowledge to teach language and its structure is complex. Providing in-service training courses and suitable teaching materials on grammar, and other aspects of language, would not necessarily provide a simple solution. The Kingman Committee recommended that a National Language Project be established and that a nationally devised, administered and funded scheme be set up whereby those with relevant expertise would provide training for 'selected staff in institutions where relevant expertise does not exist and, for selected staff in schools, such training to be mandatory for at least one member of staff in every school' (DES, 1988, p. 70). These two recommendations were realized in the project that later became known as the Language in the National Curriculum (LINC) project, which was funded by the DES between 1989 and 1992. The suppression of the training materials for teachers was a part of the political agenda of the pressure groups that advised ministers and guided the formation of policy. In effect, the LINC project was limited because few teachers had access to the training materials. In short, an opportunity to widen the knowledge base of teachers, in both secondary and primary schools, about the structure and workings of language, and to ensure a principled and systematic approach to its teaching to pupils, was lost. In 1992 and 1993, English teachers in secondary schools remarked that the project had had little practical impact:

> The LINC project had little effect here. (English teacher, St Boniface, April 1993)

> I did my training last year and we touched on the LINC materials and were told that they were available if we wanted to go and root them out. But that's basically all it was. (English teacher, Aphra Behn, May 1992)

In one school, it was remarked that although a LINC consortium had been based nearby, the department had had no contact with the project:

> We've had very little from LINC and one of them was based across the road here. (Head of department, Queen Caroline's, May 1993)

A further issue relates to teachers' beliefs about the content of their subject and their priorities in teaching it. In the Exeter study of English in the National Curriculum at Key Stage 3, there was evidence that teachers had reservations about teaching language structure explicitly, and preferred an approach that emphasized the ways in which language could be used to create and communicate meaning in different contexts.

How did these teachers conceptualize the role of English language in their subject? From interviews with secondary school heads of department and other English teachers, three areas of teachers' thinking related to language study could be identified: the purpose of language education; the content of language study; and appropriate methods for teaching language. It appeared that English teachers saw as an important function of language education the enabling of pupils to have access to a range of options in their use of language and an understanding of the ways in which it could be used for a range of purposes across social contexts:

> I think youngsters need to develop the skill of differentiating registers. I don't think they have difficulty in that ... and need to understand the different speech communities and the place of English in the world family of languages. (Headteacher, Queen Caroline's, November 1992)

It also included the entitlement of pupils to access to powerful and influential forms of discourse, including written standard English:

> I see my job as enabling and empowering children to be conscious language users, to be able to deconstruct language. It is important for children to be effective communicators in a variety of language modes, to recognize the value of their own language experience, particularly in relation to the socio-economic dominance of standard English. (Head of department, Tree Vale, September 1992)

The teachers in this study were strongly opposed to a view of language teaching that saw as its primary purpose the direct instruction and assessment of pupils in spoken standard English and sentence grammar. They saw the promotion of such a view of language education as political ideology propounded by those who had no real understanding of teaching and classroom life in highly diverse social and cultural contexts:

> There's a sense ... that ... the people who are telling us what to do [don't] understand what they're actually asking ... all the talk about correcting children in the playground. It's absolutely farcical. Have they been in school? (English teacher, Moordale, April 1993)

> If I felt they really knew what they were talking about, I might welcome it a bit more. (English teacher, Moordale, April 1993)

> I don't think any of us here would ever say that we didn't tell children that in certain situations the use of standard English is a totally empowering tool ... I think it is just the intention behind assessing standard English that makes us baulk. (English teacher, Tree Vale, March 1993)

The data from this project provided examples of what English teachers saw as appropriate content in language study; and there was consistency across all the schools in this respect. The emphasis was on how language is used in a diverse range of social contexts and on historical/geographical variation in language use. It can be roughly summarized as falling within two or three strands of the Kingman model of language which dealt with the communicative function of language, its historical development, and variations according to social and geographical context. A strong emphasis was placed on teaching that language is a changing phenomenon, rather than a static body of knowledge. Teachers' priorities in relation to the content of language study were consistent with their beliefs about its purpose:

> I feel that language is dynamic ... written as well as spoken ... verbal and non-verbal communication. So, I think some of the things I hear about trying to fix language ... as a sort of permanent static body of knowledge is a lot of nonsense. (Headteacher, Queen Caroline's, November 1992)

> Knowledge about language ... I've taken to mean knowledge about how language originates ... the varieties of English in Britain from a historical perspective ... an understanding of idioms, dialects, colloquialisms, slang; an understanding of the language tree, the relationship between different languages ... and how people speak in different contexts ... register ... (English teacher, Sand Crescent, April 1993).

One area of language study in which there was rather less agreement, and with which there was some discomfort, was the teaching and learning of language structure and forms. There was little, if any, reference to direct teaching of the forms and structure of language; the only context in which this aspect of language teaching was mentioned was in reference to proposals to include a greater emphasis on grammar and standard English in the statutory National Curriculum for schools. There was no disagreement with the notion that children should have access to standard forms of language, only with the ways in which this might be achieved. Also, there was concern that schools might be required to assess pupils in this aspect of the curriculum. Other than the correction of grammatical errors or punctuation, it seemed that teaching about the forms and structure of English tended to be avoided; instead, teachers talked about pupils' writing in terms of stylistic and rhetorical choices:

> Normally I take teaching of grammar on board, in context ... I correct in context, where it is meaningful. Now there seems to be pressure to learn grammar with almost scientific rules applied ... which is unreal because it's out of context. (English teacher, Sand Crescent, April 1993)

> If a child writes (for example) ... 'George could of gone' ... all of us, I think, would put a ring round it and just say that this is not the correct grammatical construction. It's 'could have'. (English teacher, Tree Vale, March 1993)

It is interesting to note that language study was talked about not so much in terms of content, which was seen largely as clause analysis and the study of formal grammatical rules, but more in relation to teaching approaches. In fact, it was clear in a number of cases that there was a conflation of content and method in relation to language teaching. The forms of language, as opposed to its functions, were equated with old-fashioned didactic and teacher-centred teaching methods. There was a strong equation between teachers' own negative memories of being taught language in unimaginative ways and the content itself:

> I think that could be a real alienating factor, if we are forced to go back to the way I was taught English grammar. (English teacher, Moordale, March 1993)

> I remember ... the time when one did teach clause analysis, I had to do it myself ... and having suffered from it ... both as a pupil and teacher, I have to say that I was never able to discern the value of it ... and I haven't seen anything to change my mind on that ... I haven't learned to use English effectively by doing clause analysis. (English teacher, Riverside, March 1993)

> There are ways of doing it without standing at the front. The moment you stand at the blackboard and start explaining, say, the apostrophe, you know that you have lost a third instantly and then you lose more as you go through, however dynamic you try to make it. (Head of department, Moordale, September 1992)

What still remains to be resolved in any satisfactory way is the confusion which such associations bring. For example, the comments above indicate that to teach directly the use of conventions such as the apostrophe or the structure of sentences is undesirable because it is likely to alienate pupils. However, the same comments also indicate that a conscientious teacher would correct errors in the use of such linguistic conventions – thus implying that pupils would have their use of language corrected, but would not explicitly be taught those linguistic conventions and concepts. Equally, it would seem that pupils might be taught about register and dialect differences, whereas the question of grammatical form, within which such differences are marked, would be avoided. A further point is that although the teaching of grammar was firmly associated with undesirable teaching methods, other areas of content within the English curriculum, such as the compulsory study of Shakespeare plays, were enthusiastically embraced by most of the English departments that participated in this research.

The majority of heads of English in the study identified language as an aspect of the English curriculum in which practice in their department was less strong than in other areas. The comments, exemplified below, illuminate the tentativeness with which knowledge about language was regarded:

I think that it [knowledge about language] is one of our weak areas ... and I don't think we are doing it systematically and in depth. (Head of department, Aphra Behn, November 1992)

I think knowledge about language ... having to look at that area ... has been good for English teaching. It has also been the most threatening. (Head of department, Moordale, September 1992)

If heads of department and other English teachers regarded the teaching of language as an area for development, or one in which departments were less strong, how and where did it fit into existing practice in English teaching, and why might it be construed as potentially threatening? In most of the eight schools, language work tended to be integrated within schemes based on a theme or literary text. The incorporation of specific work on language was seen as a challenge to existing ways of organizing the

English curriculum; it tended not to be seen as part of what one
teacher termed the 'normal run of English work':

> Certainly there is not a great deal of what we might call ... language
> about language. We're trying to build it into the normal run of English
> work. (Head of English, St Boniface, October 1992)

> I think also we are aware of the difficulty of fitting that kind of
> knowledge [about language] into schemes of work which relate to
> literature. (Head of department, Queen Caroline's, November 1992)

Systematic and explicit study of language structure would
necessitate a shift away from normative ideas held by teachers
about the subject. In particular, it would necessitate a change in
the attitudes and beliefs of English teachers about the nature and
place of language study in the curriculum and their own
conceptions of language as a body of knowledge. The relationship
between the academic disciplines of English and linguistics is, at
best, uneasy; the two subjects tend to operate without reference to
each other. This distance between them has meant that there has
been little dialogue between those who see their subject expertise
as being in English and those whose subject expertise is in
linguistics. Consequently, linguistic content and methods often
have not been considered in curriculum development initiatives in
English. If the majority of English teachers regard the primary
function of the subject as the personal and social development of
pupils, or the development of critical analysis, then for language
study to be embraced it would have to be clear how such content
fitted in with teachers' beliefs and values. If the relationship were
not clear, as seems to be evident from the research data, then
English teachers would probably accept and integrate aspects of
language study that fitted in with their epistemological and
pedagogical norms, and reject those that did not.

The more complex issue of how English teachers might develop
the requisite knowledge and, more importantly, where it would fit
in relation to their existing subject knowledge and culture has not
been addressed yet. In particular, English teachers' views of
appropriate knowledge bases for teaching generally do not include
the study of the forms and structures of language. They disagreed
not only with the narrow and dogmatic curriculum proposals

supported by government ministers at the time, but also with linguists who might wish to see language taught in a more coherent and systematic way in schools in England and Wales. The latter conflict is less dramatic and it is certainly less clearly articulated either by the English teaching profession or by academic linguists. The answers put forward so far have focused on adding more language study to the now statutory curriculum. They have largely ignored the more complex issues of where language study fits into the academic training and professional culture of prospective teachers, the relationship between linguistic knowledge and English as an academic subject, and the primary purpose of English in the school curriculum.

There is still a need to develop a positive and principled approach to language education in the English curriculum of schools in Britain – one that combines analysis of the different ways in which and purposes for which English is used with rigorous linguistic description and analysis. It is clear from past experience that this cannot be achieved simply by political means, such as adding a compulsory element of language study to the English curriculum, or a requirement for pupils to learn grammar and spoken standard English. Nor can it be achieved by providing a basic level of in-service training for English teachers to enhance their knowledge about language.

This chapter has indicated some of the reasons why questions about the place of language study in the English curriculum have remained unresolved and have been a source of controversy throughout this century. Over a substantial period of time, much of the debate about English in the media has centred on criticizing teachers and schools. The assumption has been that progressive teaching methods were to blame for pupils' apparent lack of knowledge; by implication, if teachers resorted once again to old-fashioned methods of teaching grammar and standard English, all would be well. Careful examination of the evidence from committees of inquiry and HMI documents over a number of decades shows this assumption to be at best naive. Debates about the place of language in the English curriculum in schools have changed very little since the early years of the twentieth century, and the central issue has remained the same: the difference between prescriptive and descriptive approaches to language. It is unlikely to be resolved in the future without an acknowledgement of different perspectives and their origins, and a balanced discussion of all the issues. Clearly, the experience of implementation of the National Curriculum shows that the support of teachers is essential in reaching such a resolution. A further point is that the place of language study in both primary and secondary schools needs to be agreed with reference to the rest of the English curriculum, taking account of what teachers believe to be the most important purposes and content of such a curriculum.

# 6

# English in primary schools

This chapter examines the place of English in primary schools in England and Wales, for children from 5 to 11 years of age. In particular, it outlines the main aims of English in the primary phase, how it is taught, and where it occurs in the curriculum. A number of issues have attracted controversy in recent years. The most prominent of these has been the teaching of reading. Claims made about the teaching of reading are examined and compared with evidence from research studies on the teaching and learning of literacy, and examples of what schools and teachers actually do.

## The organization of English in primary schools

Until recently, the word 'English' would rarely have been used to describe part of the primary school curriculum. A more common description of those activities would have been language, or language development. One of the reasons for this is that the curriculum of the primary school has tended not to be organized into discrete subject lessons with different teachers for each. More usually, one teacher has responsibility for all subjects. This came about partly because primary schools developed from the old class-teacher system of the elementary schools. Another reason relates to ideas about child development. It was, and still is, thought that younger children learn best when knowledge is presented in a holistic way and initially situated within a recognizable context, close to their own experience. The psychologist Margaret Donaldson (1978) indicated the importance of things making human sense to children. In short, younger children do not learn best when new knowledge is divided into abstract separate subjects in the curriculum, with few connections between them. The best conditions for children's learning allow them to construct new knowledge in a familiar context, and also through interacting with others. It has come to be accepted that language has an important role in children's intellectual development and learning. One aspect of this is that greater importance has gradually been accorded to the place of talk in learning, and it has come to be acknowledged that speaking and listening are central to work in English. Thus English as a distinct subject has had less importance for the primary curriculum than the task of ensuring that pupils extended and developed their language capabilities, learned to read and write independently, and were able to use literacy to help them learn in all areas of the curriculum.

The change in terminology from 'language' to 'English' came with the National Curriculum – although it had been foreshadowed as early as 1984 with the publication of the HMI pamphlet *English 5–16*, (DES, 1984), which set out aims and objectives for the teaching of English in that age-range. At the time most primary schools would have regarded English as a subject that pupils encountered when they got to secondary school. HMI may have thought that terminology was relatively unimportant, and that, in practice, 'language' was interchangeable with 'English'. However, some people felt that the change in terminology marked a shift of emphasis for primary schools, and *Responses to English 5–16* admitted that there was 'a measure of division about the title of the document and what it was taken to imply. Some regretted that "English", as distinct from "language", was the specific point of focus' (DES, 1986, p. 4). What seems clear about the use of the word 'English' in the National Curriculum to describe this part of the work of primary schools is that it enabled it to be seen as a continuum for pupils from the age of 5 until 16. One of the key aims of the National Curriculum was to ensure that there was coherent progression in what was learned for all pupils throughout their school career. In short, this would avoid situations where some children might have covered a particular area several times during their school career, and yet might not have covered other areas at all, particularly if they had changed schools or moved from one part of the country to another. Thus the intention was to create consistency for all children, whichever school they attended.

One important point, highlighted by the change in terminology, was that primary and secondary schools regarded this area of the curriculum in very different ways. The subject could not be called language throughout the age-range because secondary schools taught more than just language, and saw their role very much in terms of teaching English, with literature as prominent a feature as language, if not more so. A further point is that in secondary schools, English is organized into subject departments, in which the majority of teachers are likely to be specialists with degrees in English. In contrast, relatively few primary school teachers responsible for language or English are likely to have a clear subject specialism, such as a degree in English, even where such individuals are curriculum leaders within a school. The reason for this is quite simple: the majority of primary school teachers who trained before the 1980s would have taken a general primary education course, rather than one that concentrated on a specific subject. A strong element of teachers' certificate and, later, degree courses was child development – an area thought to be essential for primary teachers – particularly those who were training to teach younger children. In recent years there has been a shift towards primary school teachers specializing in a particular curriculum subject, even when they intend to teach young children.

The National Curriculum emphasized the organization of primary school teaching in terms of subjects, although many primary schools did not, and probably still do not, teach in discrete subject lessons. The content of the curriculum in primary schools is frequently covered through cross-curricular themes or topics. In fact, a thematic or topic approach is used by many schools as a way of organizing teaching and of planning the curriculum in termly or half-termly blocks of time. The Warwick evaluation of the National Curriculum (Raban *et al.*, 1994, p. 14) indicated that the main way in which English was taught in primary schools was through a topic-based approach, although observation showed that a large proportion of English was taught as a separate subject, often with content related to the topic. History and science were the most frequent subjects within which teachers said they taught English.

Topic work in primary schools serves the practical purpose of enabling one teacher to cover a wide range of subjects. It would clearly be unrealistic for a class of primary school children to be taught by one person all day and every day, and to have their work split into several short subject lessons. Thus a topic on the Greeks or on transport might cover the curriculum content of a number of subjects; and the teachers' and school's plans would indicate which subject content was being addressed and how. One of the problems with embedding English in a cross-curricular or topic-based approach is that it can lose its distinct identity and, by being embedded in other subjects, become invisible. The Warwick survey indicated that it was rare for the explicit teaching of knowledge or skills in English to be observed in the context of teaching another subject (*ibid.*, p. 6). There is also the risk that without dedicated time within the curriculum, skills and knowledge in English might not be addressed systematically, which, in turn, might lead to pupils' missing important areas.

For example, in a topic on transport, pupils might do a survey of the ways in which each one travels to school, or the transport and communication system in their locality; they might, as part of this work, discuss and then write an account of how they get to school, or of the different types of transport in their town. Within the plan for these lessons, English may be identified as one of the subjects to be covered, simply because writing, reading or speaking and listening feature in the task. In addition, if pupils cover aspects of English within a geography topic, for example, they may think they have learned only geography and not identify the aspects of English that have also been included. Thus there is a difference between English that is embedded within topic work in this fashion and that which is integrated but, in addition, involves explicit teaching of a particular aspect of English – such as writing in different genres, including those used to present numerical information, or using the transport survey as the subject and substance of the writing. For this to be addressed adequately, pupils would need to be taught about different ways of presenting information, and why writing styles and structures differ according to their purpose and audience. They would also need to have their attention drawn to the relationship between the form of the language which they were using and its function in the topic.

In recent years there has been a greater awareness of the need to allow dedicated time for the teaching of aspects of English, rather than 'doubling up' by covering the skills, or content, in other subjects. However, this is a challenge for primary schools, where the curriculum is not organized into subject lessons. Many schools have addressed the issue through more detailed and rigorous planning and through clear specification of areas of content to be addressed in particular activities. This has brought both advantages and constraints: on the one hand teachers may be less free to teach how they choose, on the other the greater degree of direction has probably brought more consistency of experience.

Desire for a greater degree of uniformity of practice in literacy teaching and consistency of experience for pupils was apparent in the National Literacy Project's *Framework for Teaching Literacy* (NLP, 1997). The project was set up in the spring of 1996, and adopted as part of a national literacy strategy by the Labour government. A revised version of the project's framework was circulated to all primary schools in March 1998. A key aim of the project was to develop detailed practical guidance on teaching methods and to disseminate these to project schools. An objective of the National Literacy Project was that primary schools should dedicate time each day to the teaching of literacy. The proposed literacy hour would have a clear structure, in which the teacher would be expected to work directly with pupils throughout. This structure would include whole-class teaching at the beginning of each hour and again at the end, with time in between for pupils to work with the teacher individually, or in groups. The content of the literacy hour would be specified in a scheme of work, or syllabus, for each primary school year from reception to Year 6. It would consist of three strands: text-level work which would aim to develop pupils' comprehension and composition of different types of text; sentence-level work, focusing on grammar and punctuation; and work at word and sub-word level, focusing on spelling, vocabulary, sound-symbol relationships and phonological aware-ness. The project also included a uniform system of planning for individual lessons and for work over longer periods of time.

Underpinning the NLP *Framework for Teaching* is a model of reading strategy which acknowledges that a range of interrelated knowledge and skills is needed in order to become a successful reader. This includes the ability to recognize specific sounds and relationships between sounds, knowledge of the relationship between sounds and symbols, the ability to recognize words automatically, and knowledge of grammar and punctuation. Also included is the ability to use graphic and other contextual information in reading. An important feature of the National Literacy Project model is that it stresses the importance of teaching children strategies to tackle texts using both top-down and bottom-up approaches. In doing so it avoids the futile disputes and controversies regarding the best method of teaching reading, described elsewhere in this chapter.

The approach developed in the National Literacy Project represents a substantial degree of centralization and control, not only of the content and organization of the English curriculum in primary schools, but also of how it is taught. The primary aim is to raise standards of literacy in all schools so that 80 per cent of all 11-year-olds will reach Level 4 of the National Curriculum in reading by the year 2002. It is likely that such a structured, and indeed prescriptive, approach will help those schools and teachers whose practice is in most need of improvement and support. However, the longer-term impact on schools' and teachers' practice will need to be carefully evaluated and monitored. It is important that teachers are allowed enough flexibility to make the system their own, and to be creative; otherwise, the prescription of the framework may work counter to its intended aims. It is also important that training and preparation for the literacy strategy provide teachers with the opportunity for genuine professional development. If this is not the case, then the effect of a framework, specifying not only what should be taught, but also when and how it should be taught, might be to deskill some teachers in relation to curriculum planning and development. A possible consequence would be a generation of teachers used to being told what to do, and how to do it, rather than ones who are able to think for themselves and exercise professional judgement in their work. It is clear that any new initiative with potential for such radical change as the National Literacy Project needs to be independently evaluated, and to be kept open to review and revision in the light of how well it is meeting its stated aims. It will be of particular interest to examine the longer-term impact of regular, dedicated time spent on teaching aspects of reading and writing in all the primary years; and also how schools incorporate the literacy hour into the curriculum.

In the introduction to *Framework for Teaching*, it is argued that factors associated with improvement have been identified at both school and classroom levels. These include such things as setting aims and targets, and evaluating progress in reaching them; systematic monitoring of teachers' work by senior staff; careful classroom management and an emphasis on direct teaching (National Literacy Project, 1997, p. 1). Although not explicitly stated, the rationale for the literacy project, and its particular approach, appears to draw on a substantial body of research on school effectiveness (e.g. Mortimore *et al.*, 1988; Reynolds *et al.*, 1994; Sammons *et al.*, 1997), and on work in the related field of school improvement and management (e.g., Barber and Dann, 1995).

Research on school effectiveness has also had critics (e.g., Hamilton, 1996); however, it seems to be less the research that is controversial than some of the uses to which findings have been put, particularly in relation to education policies. It has been suggested (e.g., Barber and White, 1997, p. 1) that journalists and policy-makers have sometimes over-simplified the findings of school effectiveness research for their own purposes. Such uses of research have also tended to ignore the researchers' own expressions of caution in relation to the interpretation and use of complex findings. These are important issues to keep in mind when considering the longer-term impact and effectiveness of an ambitious, large-scale intervention such as this.

## The teaching of literacy in the early years of the primary school

In the Warwick survey of the implementation of English in the National Curriculum, researchers found that there was more explicit time dedicated to English, and in particular to the teaching of reading at Key Stage 1 than at Key Stage 2 (Raban, *et al.*, 1994). At Key Stage 2, the integration of English within topic-based work was more widespread. Learning to read tended to be taught as a discrete area of English at Key Stage 1 (*ibid.*, p. 27), and pupils were observed to spend most time on reading. The Warwick study made an important distinction between two different aspects of the teaching of reading: teaching specific skills for decoding and encoding written language; and understanding of print concepts, text organization and contexts for reading and writing. There are activities in the teaching of reading that aim to develop pupils' abilities to decode print. These include the teaching of sound–letter correspondence and blending of the different sound and letter combinations in English, which is popularly known as phonics; playing with language using rhyme, rhythm, repetition of sounds; strategies for decoding unfamiliar words through identifying the initial letter sound (onset) and the following sound (rhyme) in the syllables of words; whole-word recognition; and the matching of words to pictures. There are also activities that teachers use to develop children's understanding of the purposes for which print and written language are used, and how story-books and other texts are organized. These include such things as telling and reading stories to children; developing 'book talk', such as title, author, contents, page; sharing books, either individually or with a group or class using a big book – a picture story-book with a large format that can be seen easily by a group of children while the teacher is holding it; predicting the content of the book or a section of it; asking children about the content of books; choosing and discussing choice of books; and encouraging their use of written language in dramatic play.

In debates about the teaching of reading, these different but interrelated aspects of the reading and writing process are often wrongly presented as alternative approaches to the teaching of literacy, with attendant beliefs about one technique being superior to another. Learning to read and write is complex; it necessarily involves more than just recognition of letters and words. That notwithstanding, the teaching of literacy, and in particular the teaching of reading, has generated more controversy than any other aspect of English in the primary school except the teaching of grammar, which was discussed in Chapter 5. Over the years, there have been various theories about how children best learn to read and write; and there has been fierce debate between adherents of particular theories and methods, particularly for teaching reading. Different theoretical models all make particular assumptions about how human beings make meaning from printed or written symbols.

One model of learning to read suggests that the process begins with readers decoding the smallest units and building up to larger ones: they start by recognizing letters and word segments and progressively build up to phrases, sentences and then increasingly larger segments of text. Another model of the reading process regards the starting-point as a general understanding of the purpose of a particular text and its relationship to other texts and human actions. Thus a reader will make hypotheses about the meaning and content of a particular piece of written text, and will look for features that confirm the initial hypothesis. He or she will attempt to make sense of features that are less familiar, or unknown, by using information in the text such as pictures, titles or headlines and knowledge that he or she already has about how language works in relation to sounds, meaning or grammatical structure. Goodman (1967, 1982) referred to such a process as a psycholinguistic guessing game. Frank Smith (1973) has argued that reading involves more than the decoding of symbols. He suggested that a holistic approach to teaching children how to read should be adopted, rather than ones that break the process into linear stages and emphasize the acquisition of separate skills.

A key aspect in becoming a fluent and independent reader appears to be the reader's ability to process written text visually, rapidly and automatically. Such rapid automatic visual processing then leaves space for the reader to interpret and make sense of the meaning in a text (Webster *et al.*, 1996; Adams, 1990). Other work (e.g. Stanovich, 1980) has indicated that readers use several sources of information: they use the smaller linguistic units on a page such as sounds, letters, words and sentence structure, but also holistic strategies such as predicting what will come next in a piece of writing. The information gained from word or sentence cues may influence a reader's expectations about the meaning of a text. Stanovich also emphasizes the importance of rapid and automatic access to word and phrase meanings in allowing readers to make full use of their capacity to think and understand the meaning of longer segments of writing. In practice, most teachers would probably combine features of both types of model, regarding them as complementary aspects in the process of learning to read and write, as reflected in the Warwick findings. More recent research into reading has indicated that good readers do not rely only on hypothesis-testing and the use of contextual information in texts, or on using previous experience alone.

There has also been an increasing awareness and acknow-ledgement that reading involves interaction between an individual, or group of individuals, and texts. Meaning is created through the person or persons bringing their own previous knowledge and skill to bear on a particular piece of writing. Meaning does not reside entirely within a text; nor is it entirely the case that an individual creates his or her own meaning from or in a written text. The individual creation or eliciting of meaning is constrained by social and cultural norms about how language is used in particular ways: for example, a prayer and a joke are different in form and structure, and most people immediately understand the difference between the two, because there are particular ways of constructing prayers and jokes within a culture (and not all cultures are the same in this respect).

Learning to read and write is not a linear process; nor do people learn a particular feature of print or strategy for reading or writing once and for all. Learners encounter new knowledge, or old knowledge cast in new forms or different contexts, and have to reformulate the models that they hold to take account of this. Thus it is important that people have a wide range of ways to understand, recognize and use automatically the various features of written language. At the same time, it is important to have a command of strategies that may help them deal with new or different kinds of written language and types of text. An important development in the teaching of early literacy over the past twenty years has been a recognition of the importance of children learning to read and write through using authentic, or near-authentic, literacy activities and through the use of meaningful and interesting texts. In the past, graded reading schemes often made children learn to read and write words and sentences that stood alone, without a meaningful context, or to repeat words containing similar sound or letter combinations (for example, 'The cat sat on the mat') or to read books written specially to reinforce particular words or sentences, for example, 'Run, run, run. Run, Patch, run. See Patch run'. There is now a much greater concern about the quality of reading materials for children, evidenced in the wide range of sophisticated picture story-books available for young children. The vast majority of schools are keen to provide a range of reading materials and to ensure that children have access to real books: that is, books written by an author to tell a story or genuinely inform about a topic, rather than those written solely to fit into a graded reading programme.

Similarly, the best modern primary school classrooms are likely to ask children to write for different purposes and for different sorts of audiences. For instance, instead of practising writing letters in the abstract, children might learn about writing letters of thanks, or of inquiry in relation to a proposed visit, or after someone had visited the school to give a talk. In a school recently, a class of Year 3 children had visited a nearby lifeboat station, had written letters of thanks to the crew for their visit and were delighted to receive a reply from them. In return, the children were planning to write again to the lifeboat crew, to tell them about the work they had done since the visit. Younger children, in reception and other Key Stage 1 classes, are encouraged to write and use print as part of their creative play activities. Opportunities and materials are provided in the classroom, or play area, for such writing. For example, in a reception class, the play area was set up as a doctor's surgery/hospital: the children made appointments in the diary, wrote prescriptions, read magazines and books in the waiting-room, among other things. Even where children cannot write in conventional script, they are encouraged to regard themselves as writers. The emphasis is less on insisting that children practise writing using correctly formed letters from the start, than on encouraging them in what they can do, and then moving towards establishing a secure, conventional script. In the past children's play writing was often dismissed by teachers, and particularly by parents, as scribble. Now there is a much greater awareness of its importance as an emergent stage in the development of children's writing, and play writing is now encouraged in many nursery and reception classes.

Much harmful nonsense has appeared in the press to the effect that standards in reading and writing are falling because primary school teachers have abandoned a structured approach to the teaching of literacy. It has been claimed, often with little evidence, that teachers have adopted progressive theories that encourage them to give children real books and expect them to pick up the skills of decoding print by themselves, or allow writing to emerge with little direction on how to form letters correctly. It is possible that such claims are based on a misunderstanding of Goodman's argument that reading is a psycholinguistic guessing game, and also on a misunderstanding of the reasons for encouraging children to read and share real books. Such claims have probably only served to undermine teachers' confidence in their ability to choose and structure appropriate activities and strategies for teaching children to read. They have done little to further the cause of improving literacy or raising standards. There is no consistent evidence to suggest that reading standards have declined; nor is there enough valid and reliable evidence to allow for accurate comparisons to be made over time. Webster *et al.*, (1996, p. 9) provide a summary of the conclusions of various surveys of achievement in reading and indicate that, in general, particular teaching methods alone have not been shown to account for differences in children's reading performance.

Speaking and listening have come to be accepted as aspects of English which have an importance equal to reading and writing, and both are represented in the National Curriculum. Although many schools, both primary and secondary, subscribe to the importance of talk in learning, particularly in policy documents, many still have a long way to go in developing consistent opportunities for children to develop speaking and listening in the classroom. That speaking and listening is one of the strands of the National Curriculum for English has, undoubtedly, helped to assure a firm place for it; but for many schools it is less clearly developed in practice than reading and writing. The evaluation of the first two years of implementation of the National Curriculum for English (Raban *et al.*, 1994) indicated that in classroom observations, the most frequently occurring context for speaking and listening at Key Stage 1 was one in which the teacher spoke and the pupils listened, most frequently involving the asking and answering of questions. The second most frequent occurrence at Key Stage 1 was when pupils were engaged in activities in pairs or groups and talk was part of the activity. At Key Stage 2, the most frequent context for speaking and listening also involved the teacher speaking and the pupils listening, again usually asking and answering questions. The researchers noted that when pupils at Key Stage 2 were involved in speaking, the majority of the time was taken up with discussion of work with another pupil on a one-to-one basis (*ibid.*, p. 96). They also noted that there was no indication that more speaking and listening occurred in areas of the curriculum devoted to English than in other content areas.

One area of experience that has been shown to be influential in children's progress in schooling, and in literacy learning in particular, is that of the family and wider community context. The connection and relationship between home and school is of particular importance for young children in their first years of schooling. Various research studies (e.g. Tizard and Hughes, 1984; Teale, 1986) have indicated that consistency between the experiences and values of school and home supports children's educational progress. There is a substantial amount of evidence to indicate that parental involvement in children's education supports and enhances their achievement. However, there are various types of parental involvement, from highly structured schemes that involve parents in their children's reading, to more informal means of involving them in children's education. In relation to literacy, the evidence seems to suggest that it is the quantity and quality of parents' interactions with children that make the difference. Children tend to be more successful in learning the formal literacy required in school when parents involve them in using and playing with language and in using reading and writing materials, and when literacy is seen to have an important place in the day-to-day functioning of the family or wider social unit. Both research and practice in the USA and UK have indicated that not all parents are equally well placed to support their children in literacy; that parents who are not confident in their own reading and writing abilities are less likely to become involved.

A recent development has been family literacy programmes, which aim to support both parents and children in literacy, and to support parents in helping their children in literacy and language development (e.g. Brooks *et al.*, 1996). The focus within family literacy programmes has been less on schemes for parental involvement in reading led by primary schools than for parents to be supported in developing joint activities with children, recognizing and using the opportunities in normal everyday home activities to encourage children's literacy and language development. A range of family literacy programmes has been established to meet diverse local needs in England and Wales, in many cases with support from the Basic Skills Agency (Poulson *et al.*, 1997).

## English in the upper primary years

One of the main differences between Key Stages 1 and 2 is the way in which children encounter English in the primary school curriculum. As I have already indicated, English teaching at Key Stage 1 is largely concerned with children's initiation into the formal aspects of literacy: learning the symbol system involved in reading and writing, and being able to use this system with increasing independence and accuracy. Emphasis on widening the range of reading and writing that pupils encounter reflects a view in which literacy is more than just the ability to encode and decode print. By the time pupils reach Key Stage 2, the majority will be independent readers and writers, or moving towards independence. The key function of English thus shifts towards developing and extending pupils' abilities. The National Curriculum for English (DfE, 1995) emphasizes the need for pupils to read an increasingly wide, and more demanding, range of texts, both fiction and non-fiction, and for them to have opportunities to write for a wide range of purposes and audiences.

One of the most influential models of writing has been that of Britton and his colleagues (Britton *et al.*, 1975), who saw writing as falling within three overarching modes: expressive, poetic and transactional. Britton and his team regarded the relationship between these three modes as a continuum: we tend to start with expressive writing, which is closer to speech and is more personal and expressive of thought or emotions, and then to move towards one of the other two modes. In the transactional mode writing is used for the purpose of communicating or getting something done, and the poetic mode involves a greater emphasis on language used for its own sake, or to create a particular effect. The model also acknowledged the importance of audience for writing: that writers make different choices in language, depending on the person or persons for whom they are writing, and that pupils in school need to have experience of writing in different modes, for a wide range of audiences, or at least an audience wider than the teacher in the role of assessor. An important development has been a recognition that teachers and others can model for learners how particular kinds of texts are written or read. Modelling as a teaching strategy, particularly using shared texts, is a key feature of the national literacy framework and literacy hour.

The debate about literacy, and, in particular, the teaching of reading in the primary school, has largely centred on the initial stages of the process: the acquisition of formal aspects of literacy required by schools. Since the late nineteenth century, ideas of what it means to be literate have changed. The aims of the early elementary schools were, as discussed in Chapter 2, to provide a cheap, basic form of education for the children of poorer families, and therefore such schools were concerned primarily with teaching the basic skills of reading and writing. The emphasis in society has changed, and it is no longer regarded as adequate for pupils to acquire only the basic ability to read and write. They are expected to be able to use and apply their skills in reading and writing in a wide range of ways.

Information handling is a fundamental aspect of literacy in the latter years of the twentieth century. And handling and sifting information refers not only to information that is presented as continuous written text, but also to combinations of visual images and writing. Pupils need to be able to use reading and writing in a wide range of ways in order to learn. As a consequence, there has been an increasing concern that pupils in primary schools should develop the ability to analyse and evaluate a range of texts, including non-fiction. The National Curriculum requires that pupils know about and can use different sources of information, such as databases and libraries, and can retrieve and collate information. However, evidence from HMI surveys and from research (e.g. Lunzer and Gardner, 1979; Southgate, *et al.*, 1981; DES, 1978) has indicated that the teaching of more sophisticated aspects of reading and writing, beyond pupils' initial acquisition and independent use of literacy, has been less consistent in the upper years of primary schools. It was suggested in the 1978 HMI report that a limited range of writing, and a considerable degree of copying other than original composition, was set for pupils in the upper primary years. Similar issues were also identified by the National Writing Project in the late 1980s. From the evidence, it seemed clear that more attention needed to be given to ways of extending pupils' experience and control of literacy in a wide range of contexts in the upper junior years of primary school. The Warwick survey of schools used the phrase 'more advanced reading skills' (Raban *et al.*, 1994) to cover reading strategies such as gathering relevant information for a particular purpose and selecting information using a range of strategies, such as skimming, scanning and close reading of books, other printed materials and electronic sources of information. It also included pupils' making notes from their reading of texts and using the notes for particular purposes, collating and evaluating information, contrasting the information found in different sources and presenting an informed point of view based on their evaluations. The Warwick researchers found that although schools did address the more advanced reading skills, these tended to be covered within an activity rather than being taught as discrete skills. They also emphasized that information-handling skills and advanced reading needed to be addressed explicitly rather than its being assumed that pupils would learn those abilities simply through undertaking research for a topic.

Pupils' actual experience of a range of writing and reading in school, particularly at Key Stage 2, also relates to work undertaken within the whole curriculum. Writing underpins much learning in subject areas other than English. For example, some forms of writing, such as making lists and notes, and reporting events and observations, are frequently undertaken as part of cross-curricular work in the upper primary years. The surveys of language performance in schools undertaken for the Assessment of Performance Unit in the early 1980s (Gorman *et al.*, 1984) found that narrative writing tended to dominate in primary schools. An HMI survey found that pupils were given few opportunities to develop the skills of constructing arguments in writing (DES, 1991). As a consequence of this awareness, and also because of the requirements of the National Curriculum, there has been greater interest recently in encouraging pupils to develop skill in a wider range of writing types. There has also been a move towards identifying and teaching the structure and organization of particular kinds of text. Much of this work was undertaken in Australia by researchers who are often known as genre theorists (e.g. Christie, 1987). It is often within the teaching of different forms of writing that work on the structure of language occurs: for example, in relation to words and sentences and also the organization of longer stretches of text. A specific example of this might be teaching about the use of verb tenses, the use of direct and indirect speech as indicated by quotation marks, paragraph structuring, or the structure of narratives or other kinds of texts.

The Warwick survey also reported that primary schools taught a range of literature in the upper primary years, but tended to integrate it within a topic or theme, over a term or half a term. It was noted that teachers at Key Stage 2 tended to see the teaching of literature as predominantly concerned with developing the habit of reading rather than teaching particular texts (Raban *et al.*, 1994, p. 37). Schools tended to allocate a period of time every day or week to individual reading, in which pupils chose books from the class or school library, or from home. The degree to which teachers monitored this individual reading varied: some teachers kept records of the books that individual pupils read, whereas others kept none. Few schools used sets of books with a whole class or with groups of pupils. Where a class shared the reading of a particular book, story or poem, it tended to be done by the teacher reading aloud and the class listening, without having a copy of the text to follow. The predominant mode in which children read fiction and poetry was individually or in pairs.

Literary texts tended to be read as a stimulus for discussion, or other work, such as a topic, rather than studied as texts in their own right. This was found to be a major difference between the teaching of English in primary and secondary schools.

English as a subject in the primary school is, in many respects, less clearly drawn than in the curriculum of secondary schools. Its purpose changes from the early years of Key Stage 1, where the aim is to introduce all children to the requirements of formal schooled literacy and to ensure that they are independent readers and writers, to the later years of primary schools, where children are expected to develop skill in, and understanding of, how to make use of spoken and written language for a range of purposes in a variety of contexts. The structure and organization of teaching in the primary school allow for the development of cross-curricular work, and offer opportunities for aspects of spoken and written English to be related to the content of other subjects. However, a key challenge in the cross-curricular topic approach is to ensure that those aspects of English are addressed explicitly within it, so that pupils are aware of, and can use effectively, the structures of particular types of writing. Equally, it is important that older children in primary schools are given opportunities to develop analytic and evaluative skill in reading a wide range of different material, both fiction and non-fiction. The topic approach to organizing curriculum content in the primary school has come under attack. The document *Curriculum Organisation and Classroom Practice in Primary Schools* (DES, 1992), often referred to as the 'Three Wise Men' report, suggested that greater subject specialism in the upper primary years might be beneficial to pupils. However, it did not address the place and status of separate subjects within the primary school curriculum. In summary, the focus of English in primary schools is on the development and extension of formal literacy, and the development and use of talk to promote learning. The National Curriculum attempted to make provision for smooth progression from Key Stage 2 to Key Stage 3 – which, in theory, should have allowed for the experience of English in primary and secondary schools to be closer. In practice, there is probably still a large difference in the aims, priorities and practices of primary and secondary schools in this subject.

# 7

# English in secondary schools

## The transition from primary to secondary school

When pupils move from primary to secondary school at the age of 11 or 12, they experience changes in many aspects of their school life. One of these involves the way in which the curriculum is organized. In the primary school, pupils will most probably have been taught by one class teacher for all areas of the curriculum. A considerable amount of work will have been organized around a cross-curricular topic or theme. By contrast, the curriculum in almost all secondary schools is organized into distinct and clearly marked subjects, each with an allotted time on the timetable and a separate teacher, usually a specialist in that subject. Although many primary schools do teach elements of English separately – particularly reading – pupils will not necessarily have been taught in lessons that were called English. For them, the move to secondary school will be the first time that they have encountered English being taught in such a way. The transition from primary to secondary school entails discontinuity for many 11- or 12-year-olds, even though primary and secondary schools now tend to work together to ensure as smooth a transfer as possible. However, it is often the case that teachers responsible for English in the lower years of secondary school may have little, if any, experience or detailed understanding of how pupils have worked before, and what they achieved in the primary school. It has often been suggested that pupils would achieve more in the first years of secondary school if schools and teachers had a clearer idea of the organization and delivery of the primary school curriculum – in particular, an understanding of how pupils were taught, the things that they found difficult or easy, and what they had achieved on leaving the primary school.

The National Curriculum does not make a division between primary and secondary phases, but is organized into four Key Stages, each representing one of the main phases of schooling. One of its aims was to provide a continuous and coherent curriculum for pupils from when they are 5 until they are 16. In theory, this should have made the transition from one stage of schooling to another much smoother, but in practice it has not eradicated the gap between primary and secondary schools. The organization of secondary schools has changed little to diminish the difference for pupils transferring from primary school. One of the reasons for this is that they are organized into subject departments, each having particular staff and usually a clear identity within the school. In many secondary schools, subject departments are located in specific spaces within the school buildings and thus also have a territorial identity.

Another important difference for pupils' experience of English, when they move to secondary school, is the greater emphasis on using shared literary texts in English, and in the use of literary texts as the focus for work, or as part of a thematic unit. The Warwick survey (Raban *et al.*, 1994) identified this as a key difference in the organization of English, particularly reading, between Key Stages 2 and 3. At Key Stage 2 pupils usually read literary texts on an individual basis, or as a support and stimulus within topic work. At Key Stage 3, two different contexts for teaching literature were observed. The first involved a literary text (usually a novel) being used as the focus for all activities, including writing, speaking, listening and knowledge about language, and study of the text as literature. The second was where work was organized around a theme, usually over a period of half a term or a term, in which a range of literary texts was used as the basis for teaching the various aspects of English. Some schools used both approaches, while others tended to focus on one rather than the other. At Key Stage 3, there was also a greater emphasis on the whole class reading one book together, or groups within a class reading two or three different books.

## English in secondary schools

What is English teaching like in secondary schools and how has it changed in the past two decades? In many respects, my own experience as a pupil, a teacher and a researcher has reflected some of the changes in English teaching. I was a pupil at a grammar school in the late 1960s and early 1970s; and in the early and mid-1980s I was an English teacher in a comprehensive school. In the decade between my time as a pupil and that as a teacher, a number of changes were apparent in the way in which pupils were taught English; but there were also a number of ways in which it had changed very little. Another decade on, in 1992–93, I was researching the impact of the National Curriculum on English teaching in secondary schools, and by that time it was clear that a number of things that I remembered from my time as a pupil, and from when I taught English in a comprehensive school, had changed.

By the late 1970s and early 1980s there was an increasing acknowledgement of the importance of opportunities for pupil talk in English lessons, as well as in other areas of the curriculum. When I was a pupil, talk was generally regarded as a subversive activity – something to be discouraged in the classroom. It was neither recognized nor valued as making a contribution to learning. We did a lot of writing and reading, and much time was spent listening to teachers. However, throughout the 1960s and 1970s, there was an increasing recognition of the importance of talk in learning. Andrew Wilkinson (1965) was one of the first to use the term 'oracy' to describe this aspect of learning and to argue its importance for English teachers. There were several initiatives and innovations in curriculum development in the 1970s, which included the encouragement of pupil talk, and much more active pupil involvement in English lessons. The Bullock Report of 1975 had acknowledged the importance of talk in the development of language. The National Association for the Teaching of English (NATE) and the Inner London Education Authority English Centre (which later became the English and Media Centre) both published materials to support and encourage this area of work. Other accounts of innovative work in schools were published; for example, John Richmond's account of work at Vauxhall Manor school (Richmond, 1982). More talk and pupil activity in lessons also meant that traditional forms of classroom organization began to change. For example, it was practically impossible to have group discussion while pupils were seated in individual desks in rows facing the front, so teachers began to organize classrooms in different ways. A further issue was related to the ways in which pupils were grouped in school: many schools had organized them into mixed-ability groups, rather than streaming according to ability. There were varying degrees of mixed-ability grouping – from those that contained the complete range of ability to groups to sets or bands that reflected narrower ability groupings.

## The influence of public examinations

When I taught English in a comprehensive school, one of the greatest constraints on full mixed-ability grouping, particularly in the fourth and fifth years of secondary school (the present Years 10 and 11), was the system of examinations that pupils took at 16. It was a dual system consisting of separate GCE O-level and CSE examinations. Pupils considered to be academically more able took GCE, while those considered to be less able academically usually took CSE in English. For examination purposes, English literature was a separate subject taken as an option in the fourth and fifth years. The dual examination system effectively meant that, in most schools, full mixed-ability teaching was found only in the first three years of secondary school. Equally, the division between language and literature in the examinations had an effect on the way in which English was taught in secondary schools up to 16. In the schools in which I taught, pupils taking GCE O-level in English language sat one or two unseen exams at the end of their fifth year. In O-level literature, they did the same: answering unseen questions on texts which I, or other teachers, had chosen from the examination board syllabus. All pupils studied the same books. For pupils taking CSE in English there was a greater degree of flexibility, in that half of the course was examined by a folder of written course-work and by an assessment of oral work. The course-work was assessed by teachers, but subject to rigorous moderation procedures within and outside the school. Some schools had adopted what was known as CSE Mode 3, in which pupils were examined entirely through their coursework. However, such schools were probably a minority.

Assessment through course-work enabled a greater degree of flexibility in the ways in which pupils were grouped and taught. In teaching fourth- and fifth-year classes, I was always aware of my responsibility to ensure that pupils did as well as possible in the examinations. Whatever teachers' own priorities and preferences in teaching English, they knew that in order to help pupils do well, they needed to be trained to do examinations. There was much teaching to the exam, particularly in literature in fourth- and fifth-year English lessons, although many teachers found this practice restrictive and believed it to be educationally unsound. It was obvious that such a system did not encourage pupils to demonstrate their full range of ability in a subject. Some were lucky and fared well in exams, whereas others did much worse under such pressurized conditions. I shall discuss the assessment of English in more detail in the next chapter, but my point here is that the examination system had a strong impact on the ways in which English was taught in schools, particularly for pupils aged between 14 and 16. In a study of English teaching in schools and colleges, published in 1984, Douglas and Dorothy Barnes (1984) found that English in the upper years of secondary school tended to be overshadowed by examinations – either GCE O-level or CSE. They too describe how, in many cases, the examination structure had led to streaming or grouping of pupils according to the exam that they were taking, and in those groups for the teachers frequently to be preparing pupils for the examination. The Barneses also indicated that there was a considerable difference in the ways in which the higher streams destined for GCE exams and those who were in lower streams were taught.

In 1986, the separate GCE O-level and CSE examinations were integrated within one unified system, the GCSE, which was intended to be taken by the majority of pupils. Although there were many differences between examination boards in the organization and content of their syllabuses, one of the most important changes was that almost all examination boards offered syllabuses with a percentage of coursework, and most schools were relatively free to choose which board or syllabus they would adopt. It meant that pupils' performance at 16 was no longer entirely determined by their performance in a terminal examination. The majority of secondary English departments were able to examine pupils largely through their performance in coursework. A further change was that several examination boards offered what was known as joint certification, which included both language and literature. So, instead of pupils being taught language and literature in separate lessons or groups, there was far greater flexibility to combine the two; and, for example, to base aspects of language work on the literature texts.

## The content and organization of English lessons

Although it has been claimed that schools are no longer teaching the classic literary texts, or that pupils are not being introduced to more challenging and pre-twentieth century works, the Warwick survey (Raban *et al.*, 1994) of the implementation of the National Curriculum indicated that literature still had a central role in the teaching of English in secondary schools. It also indicated that a wide range of literary works, including Shakespeare and other pre-twentieth-century works, was in evidence in English lessons observed by the researchers. In the Exeter research on English departments in eight secondary schools (Poulson *et al.*, 1996), there was also a strong emphasis on literary texts as the basis for work in English. This emphasis is indicated in the comments of heads of departments, below:

> Our basic approach is literary, but also thematic. (Head of department, Queen Caroline's, November 1992)

> I suppose it [English teaching] is based heavily upon [literary] texts, although I have never thought of it in those terms. (Head of English, Aphra Behn, November 1992)

> We certainly were a very literature-based department ... newcomers voiced their disquiet about that. (Head of English, Christopher Marlowe, September 1992)

English departments almost took it for granted that this would be the case and regarded it as 'the normal run of English work' (head of English, St Boniface). It is clear that in secondary schools, a wide range of literature is used, from the 'classics' such as Shakespeare, Coleridge and Tennyson to more modern and culturally diverse authors.

Although secondary English departments appeared to base much of their work on and around literary texts, it did not mean that their focus was entirely on the study of literature, or that it fitted into what was termed in the Cox Report a cultural heritage model of English, where only the writing of established authors with high cultural prestige such as Shakespeare, Coleridge or Dickens would be read. The emphasis in the content of English might be largely literary, but the choice of texts and ways of using them were much more wide-ranging. For example, in working with literature, pupils were unlikely to spend their time doing literary criticism, or even developing a personal response to a particular literary work. There was an emphasis on how texts work; how language is used to communicate ideas; how authors create particular effects, or draw a reader into a story or point of view; how a writer could reveal information to or withhold it from a reader. There was also emphasis on the content of novels, stories, plays and poems, with for example, discussion of issues presented in a text. Although literature, or rather texts, was the primary focus of content in English, some teaching about language also featured in classrooms. I discussed the complexity of issues connected to the explicit teaching of language in Chapter 5, and indicated why it has been such a controversial element of the English curriculum in schools. Teachers emphasized the importance of pupils learning about more formal aspects of language, such as grammatical structure, in a meaningful context; and it was apparent that a wide range of written texts, literary and other, were used for this purpose. In one school, a teacher described a specific example of how such a context was created for pupils:

> We have developed two units on children's literature. These units concentrate on the way language works on a particular audience, in this case children. And how it has changed ... in structure,

vocabulary, mode of address in the last hundred years. (English teacher, Tree Vale, September 1992)

In this respect the purpose of English was seen as being *developmental*, but in a wider sense than personal aesthetic or moral development. Teachers saw English as having a key role in the social and critical–cultural development of pupils, as well as their personal cognitive and affective development. The study of literary texts was not used for the purpose of introducing pupils to a fixed and traditional body of knowledge, constituted by great literary works along the lines of Matthew Arnold's notion of the best that has been thought and written through the ages. They were used rather as a way of representing a wide range of human experience in the world – both personal and social – and as a way of evaluating and comparing different representations of human experience. Literature was also seen as a means of introducing pupils to a wide range of language use. Some aspects of language study, such as language change and diversity, standard and non-standard forms of English, and the concept of register, were addressed through the study of literary texts. Such an approach was summarized in the comment of one head of department who identified his and the department's priorities in the following way:

> I see my job as enabling and empowering children to be conscious language users.... It is important for children to be effective communicators in a variety of language modes.... I believe in enabling children to access literature and in creating a literate, thinking society, which may challenge established truths and traditions. (Head of department, Tree Vale, September 1992)

Many schools had organized their English teaching into termly or half-termly units of work, often based around a particular theme or group of texts, as also found in the Warwick survey. The Exeter Key Stage 3 study revealed that in at least one school with a wide range of ability, and a highly diverse pupil population in terms of language and culture, a choice of texts of differing degrees of difficulty was offered. Some were available in translation, or in two languages alongside each other, to support those pupils who did not yet have a confident or independent command of English. In a school in a linguistically and socially diverse inner London borough, teachers indicated that they were attempting to create such a range of materials to support learning, and how they aimed to use texts:

> If we are doing autobiography, then we ought to have a range of materials ranging from a classic text by Sartre, or Maya Angelou or Bertrand Russell ... with simplified versions translated into other languages – a whole mix of materials, not only to support [pupils] but also to make clear what your expectations are. [There ought to be] very advanced and sophisticated writing on offer equally as the simpler stuff to get people into it. It's not [so much] complicated as time-consuming ... translating virtually all your materials, simplifying them and using pictures and diagrams ... having bilingual worksheets to explain the fundamental things we do.... We are beginning it [but] it's the key task facing us. (Head of English, Aphra Behn, November 1992)

Interestingly, a number of schools mentioned that teaching of Shakespeare and other pre-twentieth-century authors to children of all abilities was a strength in their department. Teachers were clearly working hard to make sure that the novels, plays and poems were accessible to pupils at a number of different levels. The comments from English teachers give a flavour of the approaches used and the kinds of work that pupils might undertake in such study:

> Last year we evolved a very good unit of work on *The Tempest* [for] Year 9 pupils. We worked with the drama teacher and she did things related to drama. It got them into the text ... they got into paraphrasing [Shakespeare's language into modern English]. There was a lot of textual work involved where pupils who had never dreamed they could handle Shakespeare could work with the language. When we teach Shakespeare we teach it to all of them [pupils of all abilities and backgrounds]. (Head of English, Riverside, September 1992)

Another cited work on Coleridge's narrative poem *The Ancient Mariner*, in addition to Shakespeare plays, as the focus for a wide range of pupil activities in the lower years of secondary school. These included reading, discussion, writing in a range of forms. This particular department also emphasized the links between writing and visual forms of presentation:

109

We'll do *The Ancient Mariner* and spend eight weeks [on it] ... doing the bulk of the reading and writing ... and making sea chests and letters in bottles ... [we are] very creative in emphasis. A lot of time is given to presentation and display [of pupils' work] ... which is encouraging and motivating to pupils of all abilities. (Head of English, Christopher Marlowe, November 1992)

## The impact of GCSE coursework on English teaching

The impact of GCSE on the teaching of English appeared to have been substantial. Practices that at one time only a relatively few schools had developed, such as doing Modes 2 or 3 CSE with a percentage of coursework, had been adopted by many more departments after the move to GCSE. Professor Brian Cox also identified the move to assessment by course-work as an important factor in the development of changes in teaching methods (Cox, 1995, p. 15). Pupils were able to work in more flexible ways, and to a certain extent determine their own patterns of study. Separation between the study of language and literature in Years 10 and 11 has become much less common; and the former practice of pupils cramming for literature examinations by learning long stretches of quotations from texts and undertaking rather superficial literary criticism also seems to have ended. Instead, pupils have greater freedom to study texts in greater detail, and to explore them in more sophisticated ways.

The extent of the changes in English teaching between the early 1980s and the early 1990s, particularly since GCSE, was apparent in the Exeter study. English teachers, especially heads of department, identified the importance, both for pupils and for their own teaching, of the option of assessing GCSE through 100 per cent coursework. Almost all were concerned at government plans, in 1992–93, to change the emphasis in assessment arrangements for the National Curriculum away from coursework and back to examinations on set texts. Assessment by coursework has, of course, been one of the key issues on the political agenda in recent years, and this will be examined in greater detail in the next chapter. In eight schools in different areas of England, from inner-city London to the rural South-West, English teachers were unanimous in their support for the option of pupils being assessed entirely through their coursework. They also described the kinds of teaching which assessment by coursework had enabled in their departments. It was very clear that the issue of coursework related not only to assessment, but also to teaching and the organization of English in the secondary school curriculum. The comments from teachers illuminate the effect of coursework on English teaching and how teachers felt that coursework enabled them to work to 'best practice' in English teaching, even with the Year 10 and 11 pupils preparing for GCSE:

> The NEA [Northern Examination Board] 100 per cent coursework syllabus fitted in beautifully with the way we taught ... a strong literature base, but also increasingly a strong media input – something I have been trying to push and develop over the last few years. (Head of English, Westbank, pilot interview, July 1992)

Other teachers described how it had brought about changes in teaching methods:

> You ... get a lot less class teaching of the kind ... [which involved teachers instructing pupils] 'This is how you do it – this is how you write an essay' or 'Let's look at this poem and see how you would do an exam answer on it.' ... What you see now if you go into an English classroom are groups working and the teacher going around looking at work and saying [such things as] 'Have you thought of doing this?' Teachers want to help [pupils] as much as they can. [As a teacher] you want their folders to be the absolute best they are capable of ... So there is a lot more of teachers sitting down with pupils, individually and in groups and helping them, explaining ... less telling them what to do – that's the big difference. (Head of department, Cathedral High School, pilot interview, July 1992)

Changes in teaching methods and style enabled by coursework assessment had, it seemed, also brought changes in teacher–pupil relationships. In place of the teacher as charismatic individual leading from the front, keeping the class in rapt attention through his or her own enthusiasm and knowledge – a rather romantic image of the good teacher often portrayed in popular films and fiction (*Goodbye Mr Chips* and *Dead Poets Society* are but two examples) – teachers were now more likely to regard pupils as individuals:

> Before, it was more a relationship with a class or set of pupils, you
> might have said, 'I like my top set' or 'Your fourth-year bottom set is
> dreadful.' Now you tend to think of individuals ... so it has helped
> [relationships] in that respect ... it is a lot more relaxed in the
> classroom as well. Teachers enjoy the job now because of coursework
> ... because of more control ... and the general quality of work has
> improved. (Head of department, Cathedral High School, pilot
> interview, July 1992)

Almost all the eight heads of department interviewed during the
research emphasized that their approach to teaching text-based
work was active: involving pupils in such things as drama, writing
in a range of forms and for different purposes, and also making
things and presenting aspects of work. Other research, done at
Bristol (Webster *et al.*, 1996, p. 103), indicated that English
teachers value collaborative and active ways of working with
pupils. A questionnaire survey indicated that teachers preferred an
approach to teaching reading, writing, spelling and handwriting
that emphasized an active role for pupils and teacher. The
teacher's role involved negotiating work; identifying and drawing
up suitable tasks with pupils; helping pupils to plan and carry out
work; intervening to assist and provide support and feedback;
providing examples of, and modelling, reading and writing skills;
reviewing completed work; and making links between completed
work and future work.

As indicated in Chapter 4, a number of aspects of English and
its teaching have been highly politicized, and curriculum policy has
been shaped by the beliefs and prejudices of an influential minority
of right-wing campaigners. In particular, agencies such as OFSTED
(Office for Standards in Education) have been particularly vocal in
making claims about the benefits of whole-class teaching and the
relative benefits of different teaching methods. Although much of
this has centred on teaching in primary schools, there have been
concerted attacks on assessment through coursework, and on
teachers' emphasizing individual and group work at the expense of
whole-class teaching. Ideas put forward by government agencies
and advisers about whole-class teaching have tended to regard it in
terms of charismatic individuals leading large classes of pupils, all
sitting in individual desks doing the same work. I have indicated

already why this was not a particularly successful or productive approach for either teachers or pupils. That is not to say that teachers never employ whole-class teaching in English lessons; however, it may take a form which is rather different from the model of whole-class teaching which appears to be strong in the popular imagination and is probably generated as much by fictional book, film and television images of teachers as by evidence of actual practice.

In classroom observation, the Bristol researchers found that during lessons teachers spent approximately half their time in directing pupils, and the other half engaged in more individual and group-focused activity in the classroom. Webster *et al.* (1996, p. 124) gave an example of a lesson script in English in which a mixed-ability class of Year 9 pupils was studying a Shakespeare play, *A Midsummer Night's Dream*. The lesson began with whole-class, teacher-directed activity, with pupils seated at tables around the room in a conference style facing inwards. The whole-class discussion concerned the appearance of characters in the play. It was then followed by pupils working in smaller groups, discussing the appearance of characters and writing accounts of how they had visualized certain characters. The teacher monitored individuals' and groups' work, asking questions and assisting pupils with writing. The teacher then invited certain pupils to read their accounts to the rest of the class. The third phase of the lesson involved the teacher in reading passages of the original Shakespeare text, followed by pupils engaging in individual, quiet reading, highlighting parts of the text to find evidence to support their accounts of characters' appearance. Thus there was a balance between whole-class, teacher-directed phases and times when pupils were more actively engaged with a task, either individually or in groups. Although the lesson had a literary text as its focus, it is clear that the English lesson exemplified by Webster *et al.*, involved more than literary criticism of the play, or even the development of a personal response. Pupils were required to engage with the language of the text, to form opinions, justify them, do recount writing based on their impressions of characters in the play, scan the text for specific information, and read closely to identify particular words and phrases used in the play to describe character and compare these with their own written impressions.

The lesson outlined above is rather different from a model of whole-class teaching in which the teacher orchestrates the class from the front. Although the teacher employed whole-class teaching for almost half of the lesson, the pupils were still actively engaged in work and were required to carry out a variety of tasks in relation to the text; they worked as a class, in groups and as individuals at different points during the lesson. The focus of the lesson was a Shakespeare text, but pupils were neither reading round the class nor taking notes from the teacher. Instead, they were working in ways that required them to make their own judgements about an aspect of a text, to compare their judgements with those of others, to justify their choices and then to find evidence to support their initial impressions.

The activity was based on a model of literacy described in Chapter 6 as interaction with texts. It is one that requires readers to interact with text and to construct meaning from their own reading, based on rigorous consideration of evidence. The purpose of the lesson was the development of pupils' abilities to read a text; to make explicit the impressions gained from that text; and to identify the specific ways in which a writer creates such an impression for a reader and the other aspects that readers bring to a text in order to make sense of it. The purpose of the lesson here was wider than merely personal aesthetic or affective development; its content was literary but with a focus on use of language, and language change and difference. What was also important in this lesson, and in other English teaching described in the comments from teachers reproduced elsewhere in this chapter, was that the view of knowledge and learning was one that required learners to make sense of the material in an active, challenging and critical way. The teacher was less the repository of knowledge to be transmitted to passive pupils than someone there to guide, model, support and challenge pupils' emerging ideas. In Chapter 1, I argued that the controversies about English centred on ideas about the content of English and its purpose and on underlying beliefs and values about the nature of knowledge and learning. It is at this third level – the beliefs about knowledge and learning – that the lesson described above differs from the 'charismatic teacher' model of English teaching with a whole class. The comments of teachers about the influence of GCSE coursework on practices in English teaching indicate that it is also at this level that changes have occurred. However, deep differences in belief and value about the nature of knowledge and the relationship of knower and what is known have affected discussions and practice in assessment of English at both primary and secondary schools. Some of the key issues in English teaching, and the changes that have taken place over the past twenty or so years, have been highlighted in this chapter. The chapter has also provided examples of how English is taught in schools to pupils between the ages of 11 and 16.

# 8

# Assessment in English

This chapter examines the ways in which English is assessed in both primary and secondary schools. It begins by considering some of the purposes of assessment, and how these affect the way in which it is conducted. Assessment is a wide-ranging and complex subject, and on its own has been the topic of many books in recent years. Rather than offering a detailed discussion of assessment as a separate topic, the chapter provides an overview of the issues in assessing English, and considers how these have affected teaching and learning of the subject in primary and secondary schools. In particular, the impact of the National Curriculum on pupils and teachers is examined. The material in the chapter draws on empirical research studies and other work on assessment.

## The purposes of assessment

Assessment became one of the key issues in British education from the late 1980s. Indeed, discussion of the school curriculum without reference to assessment has become rare. When HMI published the *Curriculum Matters* series, in the mid-1980s, which suggested that there should be levels of attainment in English and other subjects for pupils to reach at the ages of 7, 11, 14 and 16, it was considered a radical proposal. Since then, the situation has changed considerably, largely as a consequence of the 1988 Education Reform Act and subsequent National Curriculum. Assessment has become an accepted feature of both primary and secondary schools. However, many assertions are made about the importance of assessment that appear to have gained the status of self-evident truths. Some of these are: that assessment improves the quality of teaching and learning; that assessment and publication of results helps to raise educational standards in schools; that reporting the results of assessment helps parents to make informed choices about their children's education, such as which schools to send them to and which to avoid. In the early stages of National Curriculum assessment, it was pointed out that many assertions were being made about the importance of assessment, but there was very little actual evidence gathered from research in schools (Desforges, 1992). Since the introduction of the National Curriculum, there has been considerably more research on assessment and its impact on various aspects of policy and practice.

Even at an early stage in the introduction of the National Curriculum, researchers were highlighting some of the problems associated with the government's increased emphasis on assessment as part of its aim of making schools more accountable to wider society. One of the most important issues was related to the meaning of assessment and the different purposes for which it could be used. Researchers pointed out (e.g. Gipps, 1990; Noss and Goldstein, 1992) that it is possible for assessment to have at least four very different purposes. One of these is to diagnose pupils' strengths and weaknesses in a particular subject or area of knowledge; a second is to provide pupils with ongoing feedback on their work in progress, or on a particular task, in order to help them do it better. Another purpose is to provide a summative statement of what an individual has achieved in a subject, at an end-point in the educational process, for example, at the end of the infant phase – or Key Stage 1 as it has come to be known, at the end of the primary school, or for certification, for example, with GCSE. The fourth purpose for assessment was its use in evaluating schools, teaching programmes, or even individual teachers, and teaching methods.

Noss and Goldstein (1992) pointed out that it was misleading and dangerous to attempt to extrapolate from assessment evidence gathered for one purpose, in order to make judgements or comparisons for other purposes. Thus it would be neither fair nor accurate to make judgements about individual schools or teachers entirely on the basis of pupils' assessment results at the

117

end of any of the key stages. Some children might have started school with very low levels of attainment and have made a relatively strong improvement, but still not have reached the highest levels of attainment on assessment at the end of a key stage; whereas others might have entered the school with relatively high levels of attainment, and by the end of a key stage, or phase of schooling, have raised that attainment by only a small margin. Many have argued for the need to separate assessment used for the purpose of giving pupils and parents a full picture of the child's progress and attainment, and that used for the purpose of making judgements about school or teacher performance. In order to do this accurately and fairly, it has been argued, judgements of school or teacher performance need to take account of the 'value' added by the school or teacher. In other words, pupil outcomes should be compared with what went in at the start, and in relation to other factors such as the differing socio-economic composition of schools. A concern about the results of National Curriculum assessment was that the raw scores of pupils' results in National Curriculum tests might be used to construct league tables of schools' apparent performance, without any reference to other factors or any adjustment to account for the differing conditions within which they operated. It was a concern that proved to be justified, because in the intervening years this is exactly what has happened with the results of National Curriculum assessments.

Another important issue is how assessment is done. The three common ways are through formal examinations or pencil-and-paper tests; through continuous teacher assessment of an individual's work over a period of time, for example, by coursework, a portfolio of work, or by teachers observing children and talking to them about their achievement; or through a combination of these two approaches. There are advantages and disadvantages to each: pencil-and-paper tests are relatively easy to administer and are not too time-consuming, although they test only a narrow range of skills, and usually only those that are specific and 'testable' under such conditions. Tests are often stressful for pupils, particularly the younger ones, and they are often considered to be unfair, in that they represent only the achievement of a pupil on one occasion, doing a limited task. They do not give an individual the opportunity to show what he or she actually knows and can achieve under optimum conditions. Teachers tend to use tests to get an idea of how pupils have done on a particular aspect of a subject, or topic; for example, a reading test may give useful information about each pupil's attainment in reading words or passages, but it will not necessarily give information about the ways in which a particular pupil reads, or whether he or she is able to read a range of materials. Some areas of English simply cannot be assessed through 'pencil-and-paper' tests; for example, the National Curriculum statements of attainment for speaking and listening are not testable in any meaningful way by such methods.

Ongoing, or continuous, assessment gives a more complete picture of pupil achievement over a longer period of time and in a wider range of areas within a subject. It is, however, much more complex and time-consuming, and can really only be done by teachers. Critics of continuous assessment have suggested that it is more subjective, in that teachers are marking and making a final assessment of work that they have set and taught. However, continuous assessment usually involves careful and rigorous moderation procedures, where the work of different children assessed by the same teacher is scrutinized to ensure consistency, and also where the standards awarded by one teacher or school are compared with those awarded by and in others. Continuous teacher assessment requires that teachers develop a considerable degree of skill in assessing pupils' achievement and in relating these to wider standards of achievement. It also requires skill in recording children's progress and organizing portfolios of work that are used as the evidence for a particular assessment. For pupils, the main advantage of teacher assessment over a continuous period is that it allows them to be assessed on their best performance, rather than their performance on one occasion.

## Assessment and the National Curriculum in primary schools

When a framework for National Curriculum assessment was being established, there was concern that it should reflect what was being taught, rather than allowing assessment to dictate the curriculum and teaching methods used. The framework set out by the original working group, chaired by Professor Paul Black, emphasized that there would be a close relationship between what was taught and the assessment system, and that assessment would reflect, as closely as possible, what pupils had learned. National Curriculum assessment was to be on the basis of what each pupil had achieved measured against criteria set out in the statements of attainment for each subject. Across all National Curriculum subjects, attainment was to be described in terms of ten levels. The system was intended to accommodate both assessments of pupils made by teachers over a period of time and end-of-key-stage assessments – the SATs (Standard Assessment Tasks). The combination of teacher assessment levels and SAT results would determine the final assessment of National Curriculum level for an individual pupil.

In theory, the National Curriculum allowed each pupil to be assessed, against clear criteria, on what he or she knew, understood and could do in comparison with other children, or with national norms for a particular age-group. The success of the system depended on specifying the criteria for attainment at each level, and on making clear the difference between attainment at different levels. However, clear descriptors of performance criteria are difficult to achieve for complex aspects of learning. In addition, a framework of ten levels implies that the content of the English (or, for that matter, science) curriculum should fit neatly within such a structure, and that progression within that subject should be linear and straightforward. Obviously, in English there were going to be very real problems with such an assessment framework: people do not learn aspects of language in a clear linear order, or even in a particular sequence. The process is rather more complex than this model would suggest. A further point is that by the time children arrive at school, they usually have a competent command of spoken English, although most have yet to learn the conventions of formal schooled literacy. It is some of these problems that have made the National Curriculum and its assessment in English a lengthy and complex procedure.

In the past, when many children took the eleven-plus

examination, tests were needed for the purpose of selecting children for the different types of school: usually secondary modern or grammar schools. The basis of such selection was often pupils' performance in tests in arithmetic and in English. The English tests normally included comprehension passages and word meaning exercises and the completion of some writing, with a title such as 'The most exciting day of my life'. Since the abolition of the eleven-plus in most areas of the country, primary schools have tended to move away from these practices, but still conduct tests for their own purposes or to provide information when children transfer from infant to junior, or junior to secondary, school. Gipps (1990) suggests that assessment in primary schools is not an innovation resulting from the National Curriculum. She argues that, in addition to tests, there have always been informal ways in which primary schools assessed pupils. And within schools and across areas there were, and still are, differences in approaches to assessment. Before the National Curriculum, it was more likely to be the case that teachers developed their own approaches, and that teachers' assessments were not always recorded or formalized with detailed evidence of pupils' attainment.

Gipps (*ibid.*) also indicates that there are a number of problems with informal systems of assessment conducted largely on the basis of teachers' intuitive judgements. One of the most obvious, but also the most important, is the notion of the 'self-fulfilling prophecy': that pupils do as well as teachers expect of them. In a research study that I conducted on informal teacher assessment at Key Stage 2, teachers made comments which showed that they had tended to do this even before the formalization of assessment procedures (Poulson, 1992). In particular, a teacher in a small rural school, where children could be in the same class for four years, pointed out that it was easy for teachers to make assumptions about children when they had taught them for such a long period of time.

> There's a big danger, particularly in a small school, that because you know the children very well, you can think that you don't actually need to record the day-to-day things because you are going to have them for four years. (Headteacher of a small rural school, in Poulson, 1992, p. 7)

An important point about informal assessment is that, when teachers are observing children's performance in the classroom, or considering aspects of work, they are less likely to be influenced by previous judgement or expectation if they have a clear and consistent set of criteria against which to make judgements in the classroom.

One of the most common areas of testing in the primary school has been reading. Gipps (1990) points out that HMI surveys have shown that up to 90 per cent of primary schools tested reading in some way. However, many different claims and counter-claims have been made about reading standards on the basis of comparisons of the results of reading tests – either across time, or between one area and another. The comparison of test results has also been used to make claims about the superiority of one method of teaching reading over another. In spite of this, the evidence available does not allow any valid conclusions to be drawn on comparisons of reading standards over time. The reasons for this are various: tests aim to do different things, and schools do not all use the same kinds of tests. Furthermore, there are differences between the types of reading tests used fifty years ago and those in use now. These issues notwithstanding, reading tests give only very basic information about pupils' reading abilities. In fact, they give information only about the relative performance of individuals taking the same test, on the items that the test includes. So, for example, a test that asks pupils to identify and read aloud a sequence of words which become increasingly difficult can only give information about how well pupils read individual words; it cannot say anything about how a pupil might read a whole book, or how that pupil uses reading in his or her life. It is the more complex aspects of reading that tests are less good at indicating. Tests are rarely able to test pupils' ability to create meaning in reading.

In order to address the deficiencies of reading tests, various approaches to the assessment of reading have been developed which aim to give a more detailed picture of a pupil's reading strategies and the degree to which he or she makes sense of print. An example of this is an instrument called miscue analysis, which is now used in the Key Stage 1 SAT. In miscue analysis, a child reads a passage aloud and the teacher marks the 'miscues' – errors and substitutions of words – on a copy of the passage that the child has read. The teacher also marks where the child pauses, or where a prompt or other help has been needed to read the passage. The child is also asked about his or her recall of the passage and, sometimes, to predict what might happen next, or what might have happened before the passage read. This way of assessing reading gives much more useful information about how a child reads, and about his or her strengths and weaknesses and the particular strategies used to read new or unfamiliar words. Its disadvantage, over traditional reading tests, is that it takes longer for teachers to assess each pupil's strategies.

In the 1980s, the Inner London Education Authority began to develop a more coherent and systematic framework for the recording and assessment of children's language development in the primary school. It was the intention that the information and evidence gathered in primary school might be used also in the secondary school on transfer at 11 or 12. *The Primary Language Record* (CLPE, 1990) offered a detailed framework for documenting children's progress through observation by the teacher; by using miscue analysis of children reading passages from books; and by talking to children and their parents about strengths and weaknesses and progress made during a particular year. *The Primary Language Record* included a record of children's reading and writing activities, and offered opportunities for teachers to sample their reading and writing and to provide evidence for judgements. It also took account of pupils whose first language was not English: the teacher was able to indicate whether reading or writing had been done in another language. Children's progress and achievement was assessed against two scales: one indicating the degree of fluency and independence, and the other the range of reading and writing undertaken. *The Primary Language Record* has been expanded to include other areas of learning and to accommodate the National Curriculum assessment requirements. None the less, its framework has remained the same. The system was highly influential in other areas of the country once it was clear that the National Curriculum would require primary school teachers from the reception class upwards to develop systematic forms of recording and assessment. Many areas developed a modified version of *The Primary Language Record*, and, indeed, it also influenced the approaches to assessment in the National Curriculum SATs.

Another important change for primary school teachers, brought about largely by the National Curriculum, was in regarding assessment as a central part of their professional role. Since the abolition of the eleven-plus exam in most areas, teachers had not necessarily seen this as having a prominent place in their professional role. However, from the early years of the National Curriculum, primary teachers have developed extensive experience and expertise in assessment, and have developed sophisticated forms of moderating pupils' achievement. It is clear that, in primary schools, assessment of English – reading, writing, and speaking and listening – has come to mean far more than reading or other pencil-and-paper tests. A drawback with the National Curriculum assessment procedure is that the statement of attainment expressed in levels from 1 upwards, does not always reveal the fine detail of an individual's achievement. Furthermore, the level statements are often used a means of comparing pupils with one another, or for comparing schools – a purpose for which they were not intended. Although National Curriculum assessment, with its attendant SATs in reading and writing, and teacher assessments in speaking and listening, as well as reading and writing, may seem somewhat complex to people not involved in primary teaching, it does offer a fairer and more balanced picture of what children are able to do in all aspects of English.

### Assessment of English in secondary schools

Chapter 7 examined how English teaching in secondary schools has developed and changed over the past twenty years or so. One of the important factors influencing that change was the establishment of the GCSE: a common exam for all pupils at 16, which allowed for a large proportion of continuous assessment by coursework in English, and in which some examination boards made provision for joint certification of English language and literature. The previous chapter gave examples of how teachers thought that practice in English teaching had developed in response to continuous assessment in GCSE English. There was also a strong awareness of the ways in which it gave a wider range of pupil access to qualifications. Some teachers talked about this in terms of pupil entitlement, whereas others indicated that the success made possible by continuous assessment had raised pupils' aspirations to continue in further education after 16. One English teacher indicated that he believed that GCSE English assessed by 100 per cent coursework had almost been a 'victim of its own success' in his school:

> So many youngsters have succeeded that they want to come back to post-16 education, often, and not always appropriately, to do A-level English. But they've been finding their way on to other A-level courses – psychology and sociology have been two of the most popular examples. (Head of English, Sand Crescent, November 1992)

Not everyone regarded this success as a good thing: it has generated debate about whether assessment should be made more difficult, particularly for the purposes of certification. This rather contradicted the original aim of GCSE, which was to promote positive achievement: that is, to allow all pupils to show what they can do, rather than penalizing them for what they cannot do (Gipps, 1990, p. 87). The intention was also that pupils should be assessed against defined levels of achievement, rather than in competition with each other. However, defining clear performance criteria for GCSE grades was not a simple or straightforward task, which later also proved to be the case with National Curriculum standards of attainment. Nor was the task of designing examination papers suitable for pupils of a wide range of ability easy. The need to design examinations that were accessible to the majority of pupils, but allowed the most academically able to be challenged, was one reason for the popularity of assessment through coursework.

The whole point about GCSE was its potential to widen the base of pupils taking, and achieving success in, public examinations. In several respects debate about assessment for the purposes of certification has come full circle in recent years. Assessment by coursework was unpopular with right-wing Conservative ministers and their advisers in the early 1990s because many believed that such a form of assessment made it easier for more pupils to gain passes at GCSE, and they argued that as more pupils gained passes at GCSE, this lowered standards and devalued the qualification. The underlying belief is that assessment for certification should be made difficult, so that fewer candidates will do well. Therefore assessment would act as a gate-keeping mechanism, ensuring that not too many people gained qualifications. These different ideas about assessment help to make clear why there has been so much disagreement about it in recent years. The differences also relate to the arguments outlined in Chapter 1 of this book. On the one hand, many teachers, parents and others felt that pupils should be given the chance to show what they could do under favourable conditions, which would, potentially, allow greater access to qualifications, and entry to further and higher education. On the other hand, politicians and their advisers appeared to believe that allowing pupils to show what they could do under favourable conditions made it too easy for them to gain qualifications; and because many more people gained them, their value was thereby eroded. According to this view, the value of qualifications rests on their exclusiveness, which in turn depends on their being relatively difficult to achieve. What is implied is that academic qualifications should be open only to the few, rather than the many.

Assessment of English through coursework was intended to allow as many pupils as possible the opportunity to show how well they could do, under favourable conditions. The argument against it, put forward by Conservative politicians, was that it was not sufficiently rigorous – even though pupils are required to sustain performance over a longer period of time and in a wider range of work, which is scrupulously moderated. The underlying assumption was that 'pencil-and-paper' tests were more rigorous, and that basing assessment on such approaches would cause standards to rise. The introduction of Key Stage 3 SAT assessments for pupils aged 14 was informed by such thinking. However, it ran counter to the intention of earlier Conservative educational reform in the 1980s, such as the introduction of the GCSE, and the Technical and Vocational Education Initiative (TVEI), funded by the

Manpower Services Commission. The intention in the early 1990s was that National Curriculum assessment should involve pupils taking tests that were externally set and marked, under formal examination conditions.

In 1992 and 1993, secondary English teachers were concerned that the content of the first round of Key Stage 3 tests was narrow, old-fashioned and dogmatic. They did not believe they offered conditions favourable to pupils' achievement. A further concern was that pupils of differing abilities were to be entered for different 'tiers', or levels. In the first year in which the Key Stage 3 tests were to be introduced, there was considerable dissatisfaction on the part of teachers and parents about the nature of the tests and the lateness with which schools were informed of the requirements. The strong feelings held about the proposed tests were summarized in the following comment from an English teacher, in the spring of 1993, when there was an indication of what the Key Stage 3 test papers would be like:

> When the papers were leaked and we saw exactly what kinds of questions, the anger was uniform, and for me it has changed my line totally about the SATs. I would hope that we boycott it this year, refuse to have anything to do with it ... we would then start ... again and say, 'These SATs are not acceptable.... They are inadequate. They're a waste of everybody's time.' (Radnor *et al.*, 1995, p. 332)

The dissatisfaction was widespread, and eventually led to a boycott of tests by the majority of schools in the summer of 1993. This had the support of many parents, school governors and the larger teaching unions. Although the National Curriculum was compulsory only in maintained state schools, many independent schools also followed it. However, in 1993 many of them decided that the Key Stage 3 English tests were not in the best interests of their pupils, and so also supported the boycott. The clear dissatisfaction with the English tests, and the open dissent that ensued, was a strong factor in the review of the National Curriculum and assessment.

In the intervening years, tests in a modified form have been taken by pupils at Key Stage 3 at the age of 14. The final assessment for each pupil in English includes both the result of the SAT test and the teacher assessment of each pupil's attainment against National Curriculum levels. For those of low ability, or for whom English is an additional language, there is the possibility of doing classroom tasks rather than taking the tests under formal examination conditions. Evaluation of the Key Stage 3 tests has indicated that assessment procedures have had an impact on the teaching of English for pupils aged from 11 to 14 in 1995 and 1996 (Radnor, 1996, p. 180). The evaluation study indicated that some aspects of the Key Stage 3 tests were beginning to affect the curriculum and ways of teaching English. Teachers were beginning to teach to the test in order to maximize pupils' chances of getting higher grades; parents were also helping pupils, and in some cases asking for revision books to help them to do this (*ibid.*, pp. 131, 135). The phenomenon is widely recognized in the USA, where high-stakes testing has been more common than in Britain. Teachers focus their lessons on preparing pupils to take tests, which in turn raises scores, but also undermines the purpose of the test. This has been described by American researchers as test score pollution (Haladyna *et al.*, 1991).

For assessment methods at Key Stage 3, or for that matter at GCSE, to be valid, they should assess pupils on the National Curriculum programmes of study. The evaluation of Key Stage 3 SATs indicated that the relationship between some parts of the English test and the National Curriculum programmes of study was not clear. This was noted particularly in relation to Paper 2, which offered questions on Shakespeare plays, but claimed to be testing pupils' reading and writing ability as well as their understanding of Shakespeare texts. Teachers commented that the question on Shakespeare was a poor test of pupils' reading and writing abilities, and also a bad test of whether pupils had understood Shakespeare (Radnor 1996, pp. 107, 173). The evaluators concluded that the credibility of the national testing programme was bound up with the degree to which it assessed the National Curriculum programmes of study. They warned that high test scores do not necessarily reflect the higher levels of knowledge, better understanding or more competent application of knowledge aimed at in government policy, and claimed in the rhetoric of politicians:

Whether it is called teaching to the test, coaching for the test or revisiting work already covered, the test design is influencing classroom work. Although the average level for the age group might rise, the distortion of teaching to the test could undermine the validity of the inferences that may be drawn from the test results, both about the standards of the cohort and the learning capabilities and knowledge gained by individual pupils. (*ibid.*, p. 175)

It is clear that formal examinations are not always the best way of assessing pupils' progress. They may be good for assessing some aspects of work, but need to be treated cautiously as a representation of the sum of what pupils know and understand in English. Hence the popularity of a system of assessment that combines a balance of judgements made by teachers over a longer period of time, in a range of tasks, with tests that are marked externally. A further important point made in the Key Stage 3 test evaluation report is that there needs to be coherence in the expression of curriculum aims in English all the way through the school system for pupils aged from 5 to 16. The debates about assessment are likely to continue, particularly while there is still a concern to raise standards of achievement in schools. It is probably true to say that there is a greater awareness of assessment issues in schools nowadays. Teachers in both primary and secondary schools have gained substantial experience and expertise in recording, assessment and reporting techniques. None the less, caution needs to be exercised in relation to placing so much emphasis on assessment. Skilful assessment, recording and reporting do not, in themselves, raise standards of achievement.

'Raising standards in education' has become one of the key phrases in education during the last years of the twentieth century. It is also a symbolic phrase, to which there is attached much emotional significance. Its symbolic nature may obscure the need to consider ends as well as means in raising standards. That is, exactly what do we mean by raising standards in English: raised to where; in which aspects; and for what purpose? The key question is how we map out a future direction for standards in literacy, and how English as a discipline and school subject will contribute to this endeavour.

# 9

# Beyond controversy

## The purpose of English in the twenty-first century

The debates and controversies about English discussed in this book have been consistently influenced by concerns about literacy and levels of literacy of the population of Great Britain. Concern about literacy has, however, tended to be expressed in terms of standards falling, or levels of literacy among the population being inadequate to meet the demands of late-twentieth-century life. I argued in an earlier chapter that concern about the state of literacy, and of the language itself, is not the exclusive concern of the 1990s. It is something that has often accompanied times of economic uncertainty and social change. English language and literature have also had a symbolic role, in that they have contributed to a concept of nationhood and national identity, both within Britain and throughout the rest of the world.

The sociologist Anthony Giddens (1991) has argued that, as traditional forms of social organization and relationships change in the late twentieth century, there is a dilemma between authority and uncertainty. In many aspects of life there are no *determinant* authorities, but numerous *claimants* to authority. This certainly appears to have been the case with education generally in the past two decades, and particularly in relation to English. There has been no shortage of claimants to authority. These have included government curriculum, assessment and inspection agencies, many of which seem to have identified authority with control over schools' and teachers' work. Frequently, such claimants to authority have attempted to assert themselves as determinant authorities. Alternative views have been stifled, and many who questioned the political and educational orthodoxy were labelled as holding discredited progressive views, and held to be responsible

130

for the decline in education. The denigration of any ideas, beliefs or values that challenge those of claimants to authority is one way in which possible alternatives may be excluded from serious consideration. The terms 'progressive' and 'traditional' have been represented as polarities in describing educational practices, teaching methods and the content of the English and Welsh curriculum. Paradoxically, many ideas which have been labelled progressive are actually very old-fashioned and of long standing in educational thinking. One of the most critical aspects of the anti-progressive discourse has been the way in which a word that in the past denoted desirable qualities of progress, improvement and evolution has come to act as a political symbol. *Progressive* – and it is always used as an adjectival form, rather than as the root noun, progress – has been set in opposition to that which is *traditional*. Tradition, and things traditional, have been equated with certainty, success and, most of all, authority, whereas the word actually means the beliefs, values, customs and knowledge transmitted orally from one generation to another. It is interesting to examine the development of *traditional* as a concept in the marketing and sale of products as diverse as housing developments and fruitcake, in which it has come to act as a powerful subliminal keyword. The association between the word 'traditional' and positive and desirable qualities has been constantly reinforced in advertising. Yet it can equally be used to describe practices, attitudes and beliefs that are rigid, narrow and outdated.

Those who claim to uphold a traditional perspective on English and literacy have equated such a position with emphasis on basic skills and familiarity with key works of literature. Valuing basic skills in literacy has been represented as the prerogative of those who uphold so-called traditional views and values, whereas anyone of a progressive persuasion is represented as disregarding the importance of basic skills. In many respects, the attempt to equate a particular set of values and beliefs about literacy, and education more generally, with an emphasis on basic skills has been defensive. It has also diverted attention from other highly important issues in relation to the role and purpose of English in the school curriculum and its relationship with literacy. Howard Gardner (1993, p. 188) suggests that, in addition to needing basic

131

skills in literacy, people also need to know when to invoke them and to have the inclination to do so productively in their daily lives. He points out that, although the acquisition of basic skills requires a considerable degree of drill and discipline, the imposition of a strict classroom regime does not, in itself, suffice in enabling people to become actively literate. The provision of contexts in which it makes sense to deploy these skills is also important. School children often have little sense of why they should read or write in the ways prescribed in school. Yet there is a need for young people to master various kinds of notational and symbolic systems, some of which they learn without any intervention from school. Gardner points out the emptiness of the goal of ensuring that pupils are proficient in basic skills. He argues that in the USA, pupils are becoming literate in a narrow and literal sense. What is missing is not so much the ability to decode, but two other facets: first, the capacity to read with understanding, and second, the desire to read at all (*ibid.*, p. 186).

In Britain, this point is particularly pertinent in relation to the relative performance of boys in reading and writing. Recent evidence, for example, the study undertaken by the Qualifications and Assessment Authority in England and Wales (QCA, 1998), indicates that there is considerable under-achievement in English by boys, both at the end of primary school and again in examinations such as GCSE. The problem is related to boys' lack of interest and motivation to succeed in reading and writing – thus an increased emphasis on basic skills would not necessarily solve anything.

The conservative right in the USA, as in Britain, called for a return to basic skills as part of its political agenda. Yet the experience in Britain, more recently, has shown that what started out as the overt relationship between basic skills and a right-wing political agenda has become less clear. The call to basic skills is invoked by those of all political persuasions because it is regarded as having a powerful populist appeal. However, as I have suggested already, and as Gardner also indicates, the real issue is not an either/or situation: whether or not basic skills should be emphasized. Learning basic skills is a *necessary* condition to becoming literate in the late twentieth century, but it is not a *sufficient* condition for people to become fully literate, and to be able to use their literacy for personally and socially useful purposes. I would argue that central to the task of enabling people to become fully literate is the identification and specification of the purposes for which literacy might be used, and the kinds of texts that people are likely to be required to understand and use for communication. Identifying the purposes for which literacy might be used would go some way towards identifying what English is on the curriculum for. It would also facilitate a clearer sense of the content of the subject, and in particular the relative emphasis on language and literature – or rather, study based on language structure and use, and study based on texts – and the relationship between them. A further point is that a clearer understanding and specification of the different ways and purposes for which people use reading and writing in their lives might lead us to a more realistic identification of the ways in which knowledge can be transmitted and learned, both inside and outside school and other formal educational settings.

## Raising standards in literacy

In recent years there has been a preoccupation with raising standards in education generally, and specifically in literacy. Most recently the Labour government has set national targets for pupils at the end of primary school (age 11) in England and Wales, to be achieved by the year 2002. It is intended that 80 per cent of pupils should reach Level 4 of the National Curriculum in reading by the time they leave primary school. In many respects it is a self-evident aim with which few would disagree. Identifying the techniques needed to help raise standards is relatively unproblematic. These can be put into place largely through institutional/managerial structures, such as: setting targets for achievement in every school and evaluating progress in achieving them; allocating specific time-slots in the curriculum for the teaching of literacy; ensuring detailed planning and schemes of work for each school and class, as in the National Liteacy Strategy framework discussed earlier; providing teachers with adequate opportunities for professional development, so that they are aware of ways of organizing their teaching to ensure that pupils' learning is maximized; and inspecting schools to check that they are meeting targets. Most of these strategies are sensible and practicable; they are relatively easy to accommodate within schools and the professional repertoire of teachers. They are also ways through which a real sense of purpose can be achieved, and a feeling that something practical is being done to address the concerns of parents and other stakeholders in education. Yet on their own, they do not and cannot address the following fundamental questions:

- How will literacy be used in people's lives in the twenty-first century?
- What is English in the school curriculum for?
- What is the nature of the relationship between English as a curriculum subject and literacy?

Regardless of educational reforms, and greater control over what schools do, we appear to be no nearer to stating what English is for than in 1987, when Henry Widdowson identified this as the central task in relation to the subject. The question has largely been ducked; and preoccupation with the techniques and management of raising standards has served to obscure it even more. Discussion of literacy, and its relationship to English in the school curriculum, appears to have been concerned very little with identifying what young people need to be able to do, or to know, in order to participate fully in increasingly complex and globalized social and economic worlds.

The challenge of identifying the range of literacy practices to which people may need access in the next decade or so has not yet been met adequately. There has also been only limited success in specifying what kind of education system, or teaching methods, might be most appropriate for the future. We may acknowledge that multiple literacies will be required of citizens of the twenty-first century, but we seem to have been remarkably timid in specifying what these might be. For example, what will be the future demands of pupils outside school, and the possible futures that may be ahead? What will be the range of contexts in which individuals will exist? The traditional separation between the individual/personal domain and a world of work/public domain is unrealistic even now; it will be increasingly so in years to come. In any case, such a separation does not take account of the fact that people operate in a range of different domains and contexts, including family, friends, community and employment networks.

One of the changes we are experiencing is that these contexts are now less determined and fixed by time and space than they were in the past. For many people, the locus of work may not be clearly differentiated from that of home. The concepts of the extended or nuclear family are less and less likely to be viable in the future as ways of describing people's domestic circumstances, as families fragment and re-form in different ways. In a culturally and ethnically diverse society there may be a number of familial norms, not easily described as nuclear or extended arrangements in the accepted sense. Although there is a great concern with the notion of community, and ways of organizing communities so that they protect and support the individuals therein, people no longer belong to only one community during the course of their lives, as they might have done in the past. Social networks have become more complex, and more fluid. Although those who are better educated and have access to professional employment are, arguably, socially more mobile, even the relatively unskilled may experience a greater degree of mobility in relation to the communities in which they live. Shifts in the structure and nature of employment, and the global movement of investment and capital, mean not just that people are less and less likely to follow one career or professional role for the whole of their working lives, but also that there is likely to be a greater degree of job insecurity for many. It may be difficult for us to specify in any detail what worlds of work might look like in twenty or thirty years' time.

We appear to have been afraid to examine such issues and to have taken refuge in the comfortable certainties of the past. This is exemplified in the attachment to tradition, usually cast in a nostalgic way, betraying a longing for certainty in a changing and uncertain world. The establishment of English as a core curriculum subject in schools also happened in a time of great uncertainty and change in social and economic circumstances. Ironically, that time is often now reconstructed nostalgically as a period of stability and certainty with clear determinant authorities. As outlined in Chapter 4, arguments about the content of the English curriculum in the 1990s centred

135

largely on the study of more *traditional* literary works and *traditional* ways of defining language, i.e. formal grammar and spoken standard English. In relation to the teaching of English in primary and secondary schools, there has been promotion of teaching methods described as *traditional*. These often include an implicit model of teaching in which the teacher directs from the front of the class, with largely passive pupils who are seated in rows. The invocation of traditional teaching methods only really has any power when set alongside what are termed *progressive* methods, in which, it is claimed, pupils are largely left to their own devices to discover things individually or in groups. However, the examples of English teaching in secondary schools offered in Chapter 7 of this book indicate that they could be described as neither traditional nor progressive according to popular definitions of these terms. Concepts of tradition are *constructed*, and many national cultural traditions and institutions were late-nineteenth-century inventions. Modern notions of tradition are formed as much through media/marketing strategies – the 'heritage industry' – as through any other means.

The expansion of media for communication, including television, video and audio recordings, and computer technology, has had an impact on people's experiences of language and literature. Through watching television, people encounter a wide range of language use and many different varieties of English, from the most formal to highly localized and informal uses, and both standard and non-standard forms. Almost all children of school age encounter standard English not only in its British form, but also in its American and Australian forms, and they also encounter a wide range of non-standard forms. Most young people are aware, even if only implicitly, of how and when standard and non-standard forms of English are used. When the Newbolt Committee recommended that emphasis be given to promoting pupils' access to standard English in the schools of the 1920s, it was likely that some children would have had an experience of language use largely determined by their immediate geographic location and social circumstances. That is no longer the case: even children who do not travel far beyond the geographic confines of their own locality have access to a much wider world through television, video and other forms of information technology.

English is also a world language in a number of ways. Early discussions about the importance of English language and literature focused on their potential role in establishing British cultural supremacy within an empire, as discussed in Chapter 2. In the 1930s the British linguist John Firth (1964), emphasized the importance of English as a world language and the need for systematic study of it in order to alleviate educational, administrative and social problems throughout the Empire. Indeed, he maintained that English language and its study had a unifying role within the British Empire, in the same way that the Newbolt Committee regarded the study of English language and literature as having a healing and unifying role within Britain in the 1920s. He recognized that English was already spoken widely throughout the world, not only within the existing Empire, and saw it being taught as a second language throughout the world. Although the British Empire may be long gone, the role of English as a world language has increased in importance, largely because of the economic and cultural domination of the USA in the years since 1945. The whole question of standardization in English is still being debated because of the widespread use of the language across the world. When we talk of standard English, we need to remember that there is not one standard English, but a number of standard Englishes – American, Australian, Caribbean and Indian, as well as British. The range of uses for English have been considerably expanded as communication has become faster and more globalized. It is probably true to say that the language of information is English.

## English in an information society

Across the world, there has been an enormous increase in the amount of information available in a variety of linguistic and textual forms, in which English is a dominant language. The expansion of the information industry has been reflected in school literacy practices and, to a certain extent, in ways of teaching English in Britain. And there is probably now a greater emphasis on information handling, and the reading and writing of information books and other texts, in schools. The work of the Australian genre theorists (e.g. Christie, 1987) has been influential in this area, and research and curriculum development has been undertaken on the teaching of genre types and text structures. These developments have been welcomed by many teachers, who have given greater emphasis in their classroom practice to the reading and writing of non-fiction texts. However, one of the drawbacks of much of this work is that it depends on a clear distinction between fiction and non-fiction or narrative and non-narrative. In practice, particularly in media that combine graphic and verbal and auditory text, there is actually a blurring of the distinction between fiction and non-fiction, and between narrative and non-narrative. Text is increasingly protean (Said, 1993, p. 385): we have advertisements, which on the surface are concerned with information, and non-fiction making use of fictional, narrative forms. In advertising, and even in party political broadcasts for a recent general election, there is an increasing reliance on the inter-textual awareness and understanding of an audience. In this respect an advertisement may draw on our knowledge of other texts, whether these are advertisements, books, films or music, in order for the references and images contained within it to be understandable. Written, electronic and visual texts are all frequently hybrids: novels become films or television series; films become novels; advertisements are mini-narratives or extended sagas; narratives are embedded within non-fiction information texts; the linguistic structure and prosody of medieval or early modern texts, such as Shakespeare or Malory, may be found in cartoons for children.

The range of literacy practices of the majority of people in Britain in the late twentieth century is vast; but acts involving literacy are not just confined to reading books, filling in forms or writing letters or instructions. More often than not, literacy practices involve more than one form of representation, or notation; they require, for example, that text and pictures be read together to produce meaning. An emphasis on basic skills in reading and writing may well be important, but being able to sound out words from individual letters or clusters of syllables will not of itself enable pupils to become fully literate. We need to go beyond the polarization implied in the labels 'progressive' and 'traditional' and to examine the purposes that literacy serves, and then to consider how the English curriculum in schools may enable pupils to have not only a grasp of the basic skills, but also an understanding of the wider potential of literacy. We need to consider how to allow people to have access to a range of different kinds of texts and the knowledge structures and social relationships underpinning them. The teachers in the research studies described earlier in this book were already teaching classic works of literature, not by ploughing through the texts from beginning to end, or through pupils' memorization of chunks of text, but instead by introducing film or video versions. They used written texts accompanied by pictures, or by translations into modern English, and, where appropriate, another language alongside the original. Although study of media had little attention in the curriculum reforms of the 1990s, its practical application in English has been widespread. However, future discussions of the content and purpose of English need to have a much more inclusive definition of language and literature and of the ways in which they will be experienced by pupils. Any programme for the study of language and literature in the school curriculum ideally should take account of the reasons that pupils may have for wishing to acquire such knowledge, and the occasions on which it might be used. Thus attempts to raise standards of literacy beyond the most basic initial levels should be set alongside a clear specification of possible rationales and occasions for using and accessing written language in its various forms and manifestations.

However, this is unlikely to happen until we openly acknowledge that there are a number of competing value systems informing the debate about English, and that these have implications for what is believed to be its purpose, the most appropriate choice of content, and the best ways to teach the subject. This book has identified the issues involved in the recent debates and controversies concerning English teaching in both primary and secondary schools. It has indicated how underlying values and beliefs have informed different aspects of the debate, the high degree of politicization of the subject in recent years, and the many issues that remain to be resolved in a constructive way. As indicated in Chapter 3, the Cox Report went some way towards an acknowledgement of different positions and priorities. But in that chapter it was also argued that the inclusiveness of the

English curriculum recommended by the Cox Committee had some serious limitations. One of the most important of these was that it did not fully identify, or explore the nature of, the difference between positions, the degree of overlap between them, or their relationship with one another. Differences cannot easily be resolved through accommodation and compromise that do not address the fundamental questions of how and where the informing value systems may differ and be similar. As indicated in the examples in this book, teachers tend to accommodate procedural and practical changes, provided that this can be done within their value system and framework of beliefs. When they cannot – as was the case in 1992 and 1993, and may yet be the case again – teachers do not necessarily acquiesce, but are more likely to resist strongly.

The importance of identifying the different systems of values and beliefs, and the inter-connections between them, is of critical importance for the future of English, particularly in a time of considerable social, economic and cultural uncertainty. In many respects the subject and its teaching was at the centre of the Conservative political and cultural endeavour between 1979 and 1997. Much of this was backward-looking; but, as Brian Cox (1995) remarked, the Conservative educational agenda was implemented by people with good intentions, strong beliefs and determination. It is not enough to dismiss the controversies over English as originating in the policies of the politically misguided: they warrant a closer look at what exactly was intended, and how these intentions and assumptions about education and English teaching differed from the aims and assumptions of the English teachers in secondary schools and class teachers in primary schools. Finally, as I have indicated in this chapter, we need to go beyond the rhetoric of raising standards of literacy and concentrate on the techniques for doing so. Just as important is the need to answer fundamental questions about the purpose of English in relation to widening definitions of literacy and increasingly complex literacy practices required of citizens in the twenty-first century. In answering these questions, we need to fully acknowledge the globalization of technology and of cultural life, and the role of English as a world language.

# Bibliography

Adams, M. J. (1990) *Beginning to Read* (Cambridge, MA: MIT Press).

Arnold, M. (1932 [1869]) *Culture and Anarchy*, ed. J. Dover Wilson (Cambridge: Cambridge University Press).

Arnold, M. (1962) *Democratic Education*, vol. 2: *The Complete Prose Works of Matthew Arnold* (Ann Arbor: University of Michigan Press).

Ball, S. J. (1983) 'A subject of privilege: English and the school curriculum 1906–1935', in M. Hammersley and A. Hargreaves (eds), *Curriculum Practice: Some Sociological Case Studies* (Lewes: Falmer Press), pp. 61–88.

Ball, S. J. (1985) 'English for the English since 1906', in I. Goodson (ed.), *Social Histories of the Secondary Curriculum* (Lewes: Falmer Press).

Barber, M. and Dann, R. (eds) (1995) *Raising Educational Standards in the Inner City: Practical Initiatives in Action* (London: Cassell).

Barber, M. and White, J. (1997) 'Introduction', in J. White and M. Barber (eds), *Perspectives on School Effectiveness and School Improvement* (London: Institute of Education), pp. 1–8.

Barnes, D. and Barnes, D. with Clarke, S. (1984) *Versions of English* (London: Heinemann).

Board of Education (1905) *Handbook of Suggestions for the Consideration of Teachers and Others Concerned in the Work of the Public Elementary Schools* (London: HMSO).

Board of Education (1908) *Reports on Elementary Schools, 1852–1882* (London: HMSO).

Board of Education (1910) *The Teaching of English in Secondary Schools* (London: HMSO).

Board of Education (1921) *The Teaching of English in England* (Newbolt Report) (London: HMSO).

Board of Education (1926) *Report of the Consultative Committee on the Education of the Adolescent* (Hadow Report) (London: HMSO).

Britton, J. (1973) 'How we got here', in N. Bagnell (ed.), *New Movements in the Teaching of English* (London: Temple Smith), pp. 13–29.

Britton, J., Burgess, T., Martin, N., Macleod, A. and Rosen, H. (1975) *The Development of Writing Abilities 11–18* (London: Macmillan).

Brooks, G., Gorman, T., Harman, A., Hutchinson, D. and Wilkin, A. (1996) *Family Literacy Works* (London: Basic Skills Agency).

Centre for Language in Primary Education (1990) *Patterns of Learning: The Primary Language Record and the National Curriculum* (London: CLPE).

Christie, F. (1987) 'Young children's writing: from spoken to written genre', *Language and Education*, 1(1), 3–13.

Cook, E. T. and Wedderburn, A. (eds) (1905) *The Works of John Ruskin* (London: George Allen).

Cox, B. (1991) *Cox on Cox: An English Curriculum for the 1990s* (London: Hodder & Stoughton).

Cox, B. (1995) *Cox on the Battle for the English Curriculum* (London: Hodder & Stoughton).

Crombie, W. and Poulson, L. (1991) 'Unity and uniformity: the concept of English in the UK national curriculum', *English – A World Language: Journal of the English – Speaking Union*, 1(1), 9–17.

Crowley, T. (1989) *The Politics of Discourse* (London: Macmillan).

Department of Education and Science (DES) (1975) *A Language for Life* (Bullock Report) (London: HMSO).

DES (1978) *Primary Education in England* (London: HMSO).

DES (1984) *Curriculum Matters 1: English 5–16* (London: HMSO).

DES (1986) *English 5–16: The Responses to Curriculum Matters 1* (London: HMSO).

DES (1988) *Report of the Committee of Enquiry into the Teaching of English Language* (Kingman Report) (London: HMSO).

DES (1989a) *English for Ages 5–16* (Cox Report) (London: HMSO).

DES (1989a) *English in the National Curriculum* (London: HMSO).

DES (1991) *Education Observed: The Implementation of the Curricular Requirements of the ERA in 1989–90* (London: HMSO).

DES (1992) *Curriculum Organisation and Classroom Practice in Primary Schools: A Discussion Paper* (London: Department of Education and Science).

Desforges, C. (1992) 'Assessment and learning', *Forum*, **34**(4), 68–9.

DFE (1995) *The National Curriculum* (London: HMSO).

DFEE (1997) *Excellence in Schools* (London: HMSO).

Dixon, J. (1966) *Growth Through English: A Report Based on the Dartmouth Seminar* (Oxford: Oxford University Press).

Dixon, J. (1991) *A Schooling in English* (Buckingham: Open University Press).

Donaldson, M. (1978) *Children's Minds* (London: Fontana).

Donaldson, M. (1992) *Human Minds* (London: Penguin).

Firth, J. R. (1964) *Tongues of Men and Speech*, ed. P. Strevens (Oxford: Oxford University Press).

Fox, D., Goodwyn, A. and Zacanella, D. (1993) 'Teachers' theoretical models of English and of English teaching: an international comparison', paper presented at the Fifth International Convention on Language in Education, March, University of East Anglia, Norwich.

Frater, G. (1993) 'Back to the future', *Education*, 22 March.

Gardner, H. (1993) *The Unschooled Mind* (London: Fontana).

Giddens, A. (1991) *Modernity and Self Identity* (Cambridge: Polity Press).

Gipps, C. (1990) *Assessment: A Teachers' Guide to the Issues* (London: Hodder & Stoughton).

Goodman, K. (1967) 'Reading: a psycholinguistic guessing game', *Journal of the Reading Specialist*, **6**(4), 126–35.

Goodman, K. (1982) *The Selected Writings of Kenneth S. Goodman*, Vols 1 and 2, edited by F. Gallasch (Boston: Routledge and Kegan Paul).

Gorman, T., White, J., Hargreaves, M., MacLure, M. and Tate, A. (1984) *Language Performance in Schools: 1982 Primary Survey Report* (London: HMSO).

Grossman, P. (1991) *The Making of a Teacher: Teacher Knowledge and Teacher Education* (New York: Teachers College Press).

Haladyna, T., Nolan, S. and Haas, N. (1991) 'Raising standardized achievement test scores and the origins of test score pollution', *Educational Researcher*, **20**(5), 2–7.

Hamilton, D. (1996) 'Peddling feel-good fictions', *Forum*, **38**(2), 54–6.

Holmes, E. (1911) *What Is and What Ought to Be* (London: Constable).

Honey, J. (1983) *The Language Trap* (London: National Council for Educational Standards).

Hopkins, D., Ainscow, M. and West, M. (1994) *School Improvement in an Era of Change* (London: Cassell).

Hughes, M., Wikely, F. and Nash, T. (1994) *Parents and Their Children's Schools* (Oxford: Blackwell).

Lawlor, S. (1990) *The Correct Core* (London: Centre for Policy Studies).

Letwin, O. (1988) *Aims of Schooling: The Importance of Grounding* (London: Centre for Policy Studies).

Lunzer, E. and Gardner, K. (1979) *The Effective Use of Reading* (London: Heinemann).

Marenbon, J. (1987) *English, Our English* (London: Centre for Policy Studies).

Mathieson, M. (1975) *The Preachers of Culture* (London: George Allen & Unwin).

Mathieson, M. (1991) '1991 – the teaching of English in England', *Oxford Review of Education*, **17**(1), 3–16.

Milroy, J. and Milroy, L. (1985) *Authority in Language* (London: Routledge).

Mortimore, P., Sammons, P., Stoll, L., Lewis, D. and Ecob, R. (1988) *School Matters: The Junior Years* (Wells: Open Books).

National Curriculum Council (1992) *National Curriculum English: The Case for Revising the Order* (York: NCC).

National Literacy Project (1997) *The National Literacy Project Framework for Teaching* (Reading: NLP).

Noss, R. and Goldstein, H. (1991) 'Alternative currents', *Forum*, **34**(1), 15–17.

Nunn, P. (1920) *Education: Its Data and First Principles* (London: Edward Arnold).

Poulson, L. (1991) 'The illusion of consensus: English teaching and the U.K. national curriculum', *Language Arts Journal of Michigan*, **8**(1), 71–83.

Poulson, L. (1992) 'Literacy and teacher assessment at Key Stage 2', *Reading*, **26**(3), 6–12.

Poulson, L., Radnor, H. and Turner-Bisset, R. (1996) 'From policy to practice: language education, English teaching and curriculum reform in secondary schools in England', *Language and Education*, **10**(1), 33–46.

Poulson, L., Macleod, F., Bennett, N. and Wray, D. (1997) *Family Literacy: Practice in Local Programmes* (London: Basic Skills Agency).

Qualifications and Curriculum Authority (1998) *'Can Do Better'* (London: QCA).

Raban, B., Clark, U., Dennis, D., McIntyre, J. and Zalasiewicz, K. (1994) *Evaluation of the Implementation of English in the National Curriculum at Key Stages 1, 2, and 3 (1991–93)* (London: School Curriculum and Assessment Authority).

Radnor, H. (1996) *Evaluation of Key Stage 3 Assessment 1995–1996* (London: School Curriculum and Assessment Authority).

Radnor, H., Poulson, L. and Turner-Bissett, R. (1995) 'Assessment and teacher professionalism', *Curriculum Journal*, **6**(3), 325–42.

Reynolds, D., Creemers, B., Nesselrodt, P. S., Schaffer, E. C., Stringfield, S. and Teddlie, C. (eds) (1994) *Advances in School Effectiveness Research and Practice* (Oxford: Pergamon).

Richmond, J. (1982) *Becoming Our Own Experts* (London: Inner London Education Authority English Centre).

Said, E. W. (1993) *Culture and Imperialism* (London: Vintage).

Sammons, P., Hillman, J. and Mortimore, P. (1997) 'Key characteristics of effective schools: a review of school effectiveness research', in J. White and M. Barber (eds), *Perspectives on School Effectiveness and School Improvement* (London: Institute of Education), pp. 77–124.

Sampson, G. (1926) *English for the English* (Cambridge: Cambridge University Press).

Smith, F. (ed.) (1973) *Psycholinguistics and Reading* (New York: Holt, Rinehart & Winston).

Southgate, V., Arnold, H. and Johnson, S. (1981) *Extending Beginning Reading* (London: Heinemann).

Stanovich, K. E. (1980) 'Towards an interactive-compensatory model of individual differences in the development of reading', *Reading Research Quarterly*, **16**(1), 32–71.

Start, K. and Wells, B. (1972) *The Trend of Reading Standards* (Slough: NFER).

Teale, W. H. (1986) 'Home backgrounds and young children's literacy development', in W. H. Teale and E. Sulzby (eds), *Emergent Literacy: Writing and Reading* (Norwood, NJ: Ablex.).

Tizard, B. and Hughes, M. (1984) *Young Children Learning: Talking and Thinking at Home and School* (London: Fontana).

Trevelyan, G. O. (1900) *Macaulay's Life and Letters* (London: Longman, Green & Co.).

Webster, A., Beveridge, M. and Reed, M. (1996) *Managing the Literacy Curriculum* (London: Routledge).

Wilkinson, A. M. (1965) *Spoken English*, Educational Review Occasional Papers No. 2 (Birmingham: University of Birmingham).

Wilks, J. (1993) (ed.) *Voices from the Classroom* (London: London Association for the Teaching of English).

# Index